LEARN ALL ABOUT
DOLPHINS

COLOR PHOTOS, FACTS, & STORIES for Kids

ANIMAL FACT FINDERS

Copyright © 2023

All rights reserved. This book is copyright protected. You cannot amend, distribute, or sell any part of the content within this book without the consent of the author or publisher. While every attempt has been made to verify the validity of the content in this book, the author or publisher cannot assume responsibility for any errors or omissions. The information contained in this book is intended for entertainment purposes only and is not a substitute for professional advice. No warranties of any kind are declared or implied. Consult a licensed professional for expert services when needed.

Version 1.005

Table of Contents

Welcome to the wonderful world of dolphins! 6

What did dolphins evolve from? 8

How many types of dolphins are there? 11

What do dolphins eat? 20

How do dolphins breathe? 28

How do dolphins sleep? 33

How do dolphins communicate? 37

How fast can dolphins swim? 42

Why do dolphins jump out of the water? 46

How intelligent are dolphins? 51

How long do dolphins live? 57

Do dolphins have any predators? 62

Are dolphins endangered? 69

Welcome to the wonderful world of dolphins!

Jumping, flipping, dancing, and playing all the live long day… Dolphins are sometimes referred to as the "geniuses of the ocean." Have you ever been lucky enough to see one? Maybe you've spotted dolphins in aquariums or water parks, where they often delight the audience with their amazing acrobatics and fascinating tricks. Maybe you've met one in the wild. If you have, then you might have noticed that they love to chase each other, surf on the waves, and play "toss the seaweed" with their friends.

Dolphins are super social, interesting, and brainy creatures, which is why they are so much fun to study and learn about. If you've ever wanted to know what they eat, how they speak, and why they jump so high, then this is the perfect book for you! Prepare to be amazed as we discover all there is to know about these beloved creatures!

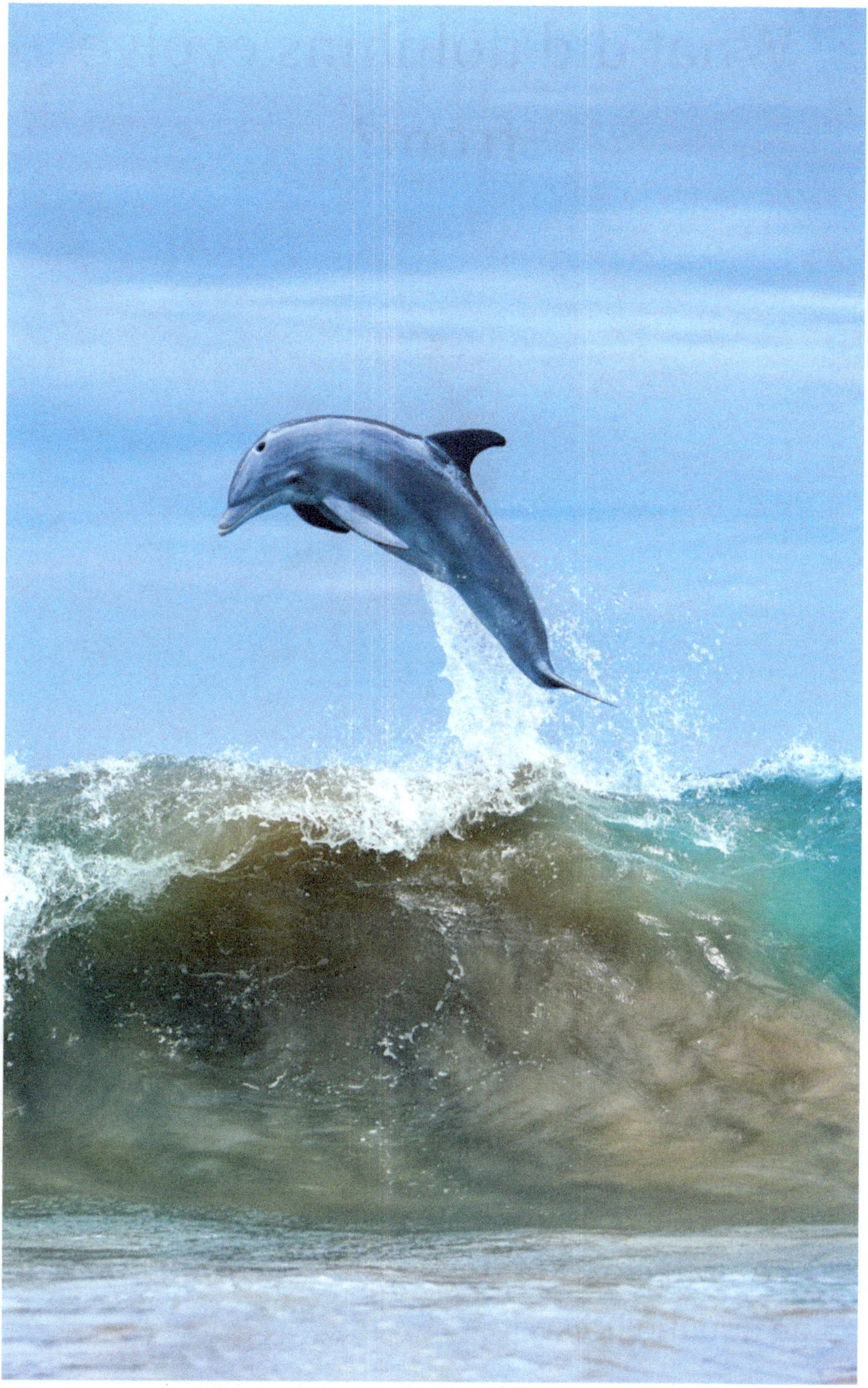

What did dolphins evolve from?

It is believed that the ancestors of modern dolphins go as far back as 50 million years ago. Back then, they looked nothing like the dolphins we know today. They were small, four-legged animals that looked a bit like a short deer. They lived on the land but ventured into the rivers sometimes. Over the years (many millions of years), these land animals ventured closer to the water and eventually adopted an aquatic lifestyle.

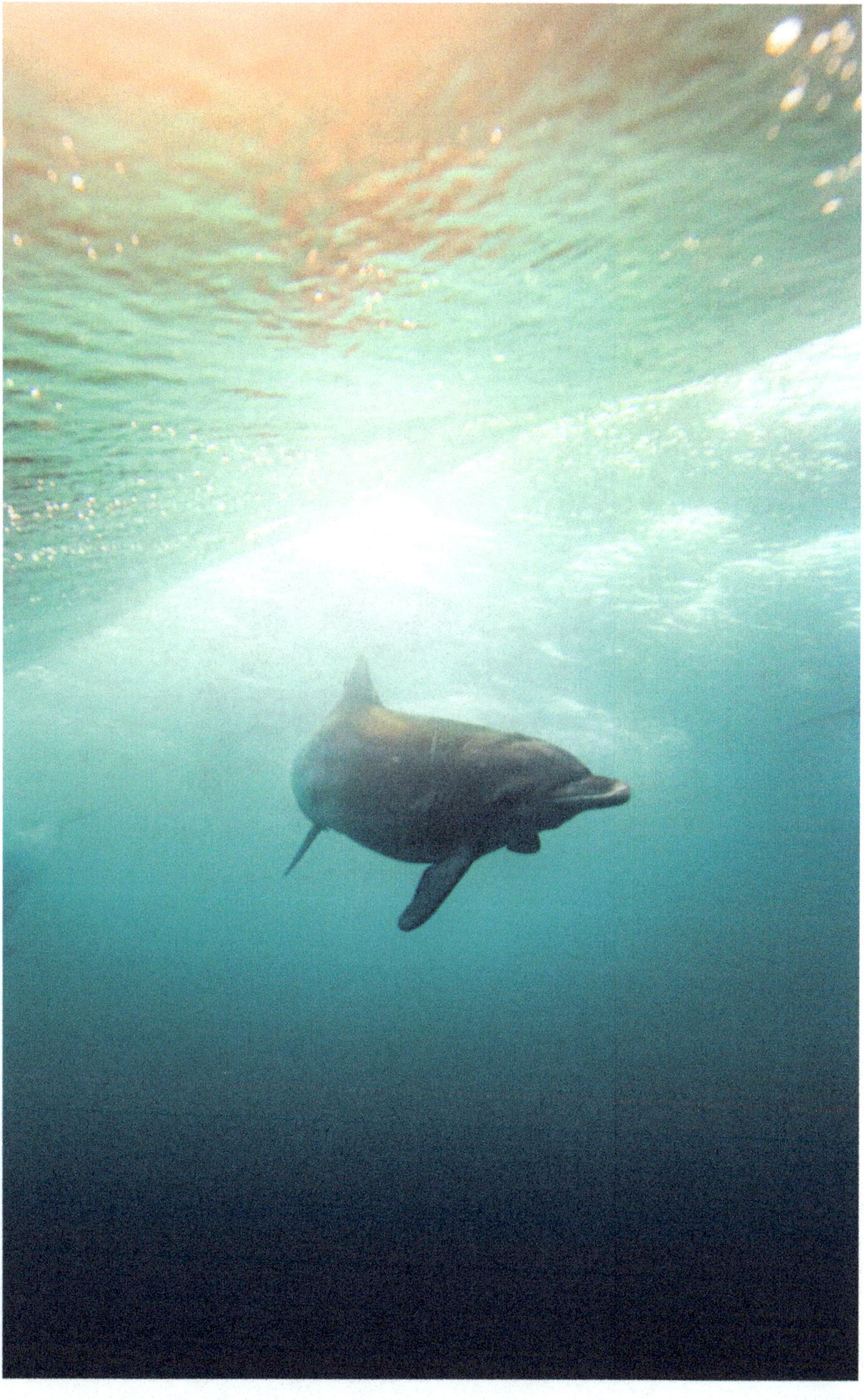

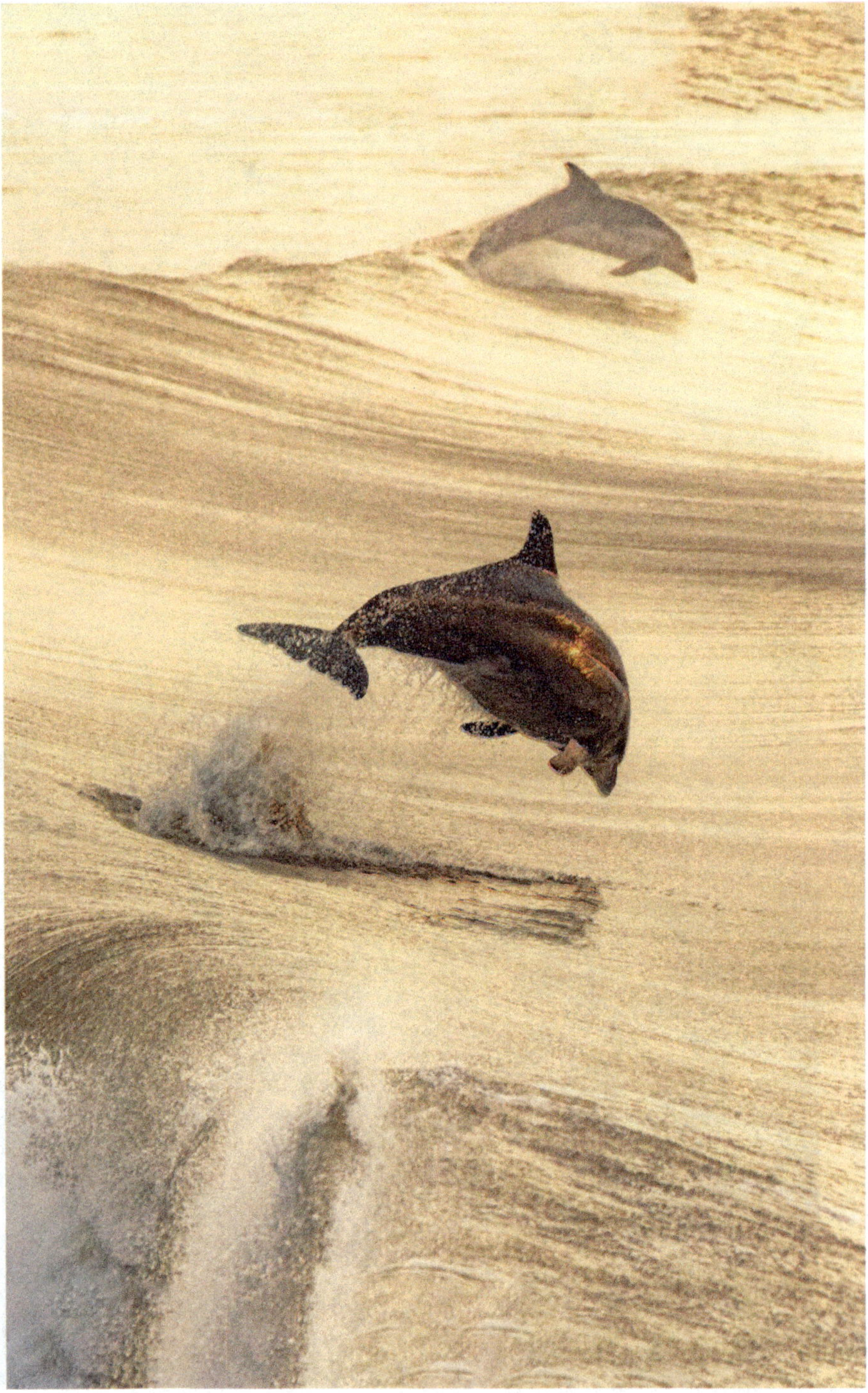

How many types of dolphins are there?

Although a dolphin might look like a huge fish, it's actually a mammal, just like you and me. We've got a lot in common with dolphins. Dolphins breathe air, nurse their young, and even have hair (although it's not very long).

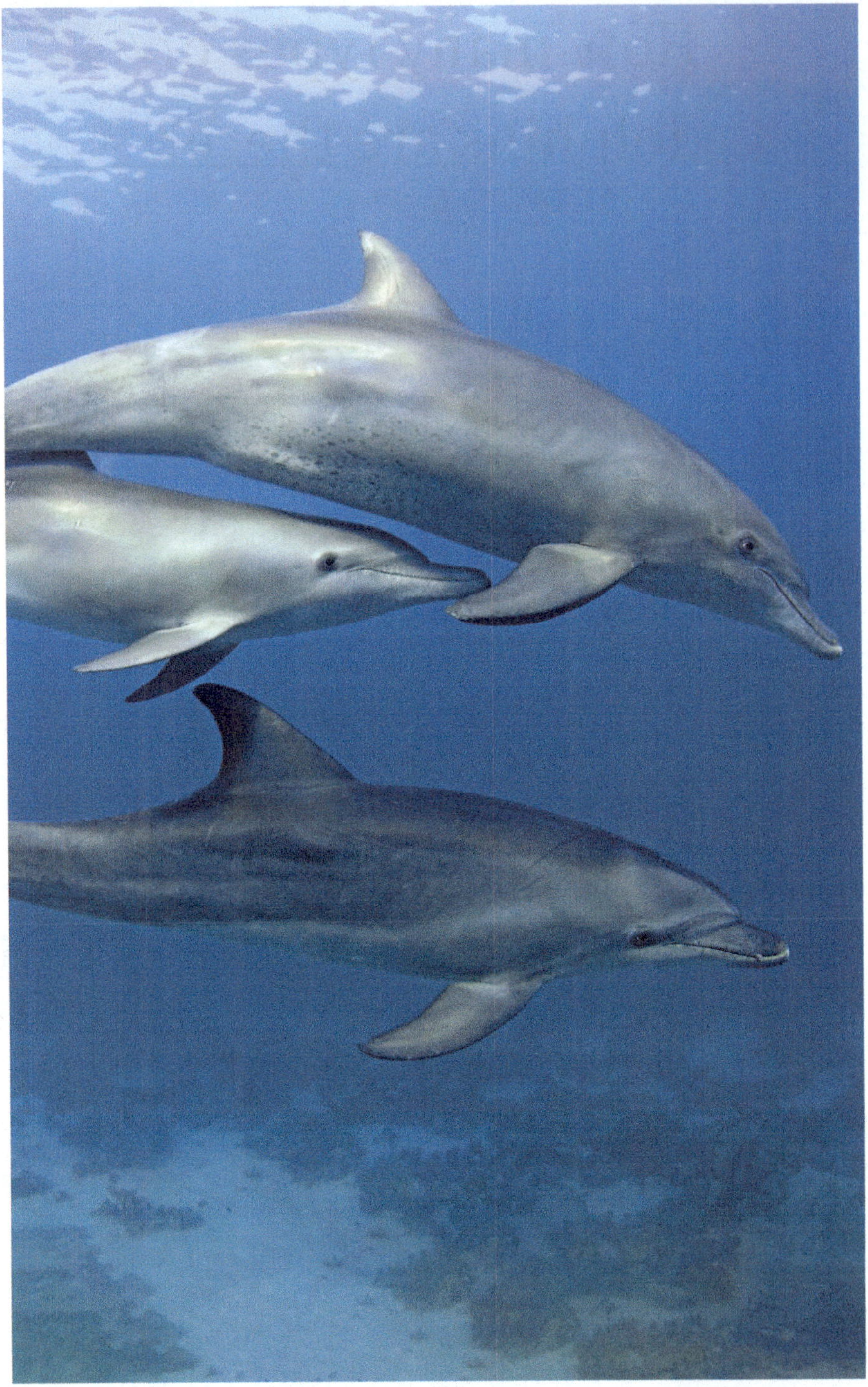

Dolphins belong to a large family called *Cetacea*, which also includes whales and porpoises. Most people know what a whale looks like, but many tend to confuse the dolphin and the **porpoise** because they really do look quite similar. However, dolphins are usually larger than porpoises, and they have longer snouts and bigger mouths, all the better to smile at you!

The below picture is of a porpoise. Notice how it doesn't have much of a "nose" like a dolphin does.

There are 42 different species of dolphins in the world, many of which have their own unique characteristics and behaviors. For example:

- **Maui's dolphin** (the smallest and rarest dolphin) has a maximum length of only 4.9 feet and weighs up to 110 pounds.
- In comparison, the **orca whale** (which is also a dolphin despite its confusing name) is a massive 30 feet in length and weighs in at a hefty 8,000 - 10,000 pounds!
- The most common dolphin is known as the **bottlenose dolphin**. Can you guess why it has that name? Because its snout (or beak) is shaped like a bottle. The bottlenose dolphin measures around 6 to 12 feet long and can weigh anywhere from 300 to 1,400 pounds.

Perhaps the easier way to sort the dolphins would be by their **habitat**. In this sense, there are just two main types of dolphins: the ones that live in the **ocean** and those that prefer a life in the **rivers**.

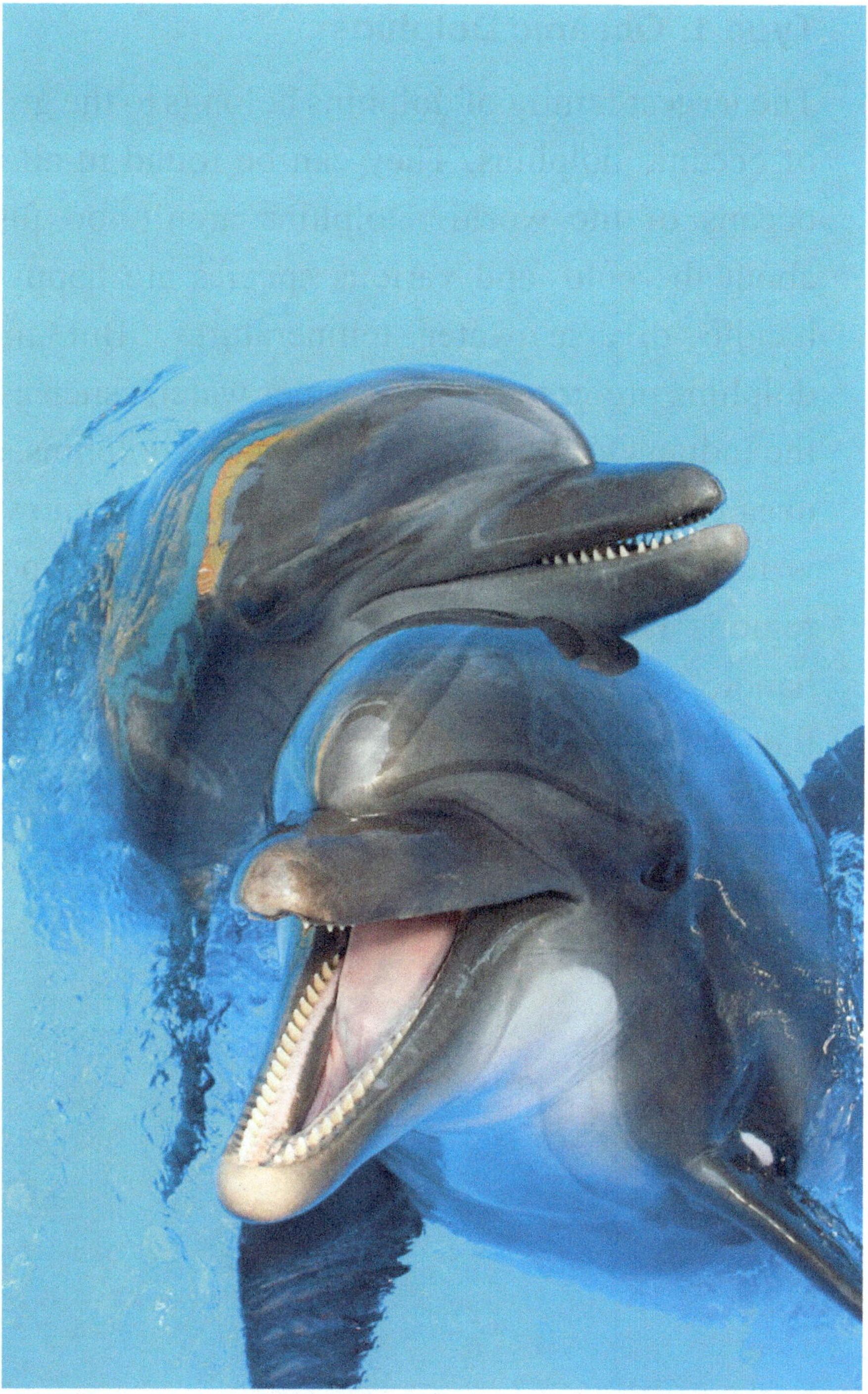

Type 1: Oceanic Dolphins

The largest family of dolphins belongs to the group of oceanic dolphins. They can be found in all the oceans of the world. Dolphins aren't too fussy about the cold, and various species are happy to handle diverse water temperatures. But most dolphins prefer to live in warmer waters, such as in the Indian Ocean. The largest of these dolphins, the **orca** (or "**killer whale**" as it's commonly known), is happy to reside in the icy water of the polar regions. However, if the water becomes too cold to handle, or if the food supply begins to dwindle, then the dolphins will migrate to warmer waters.

The next photo shows an image of an orca surfacing briefly.

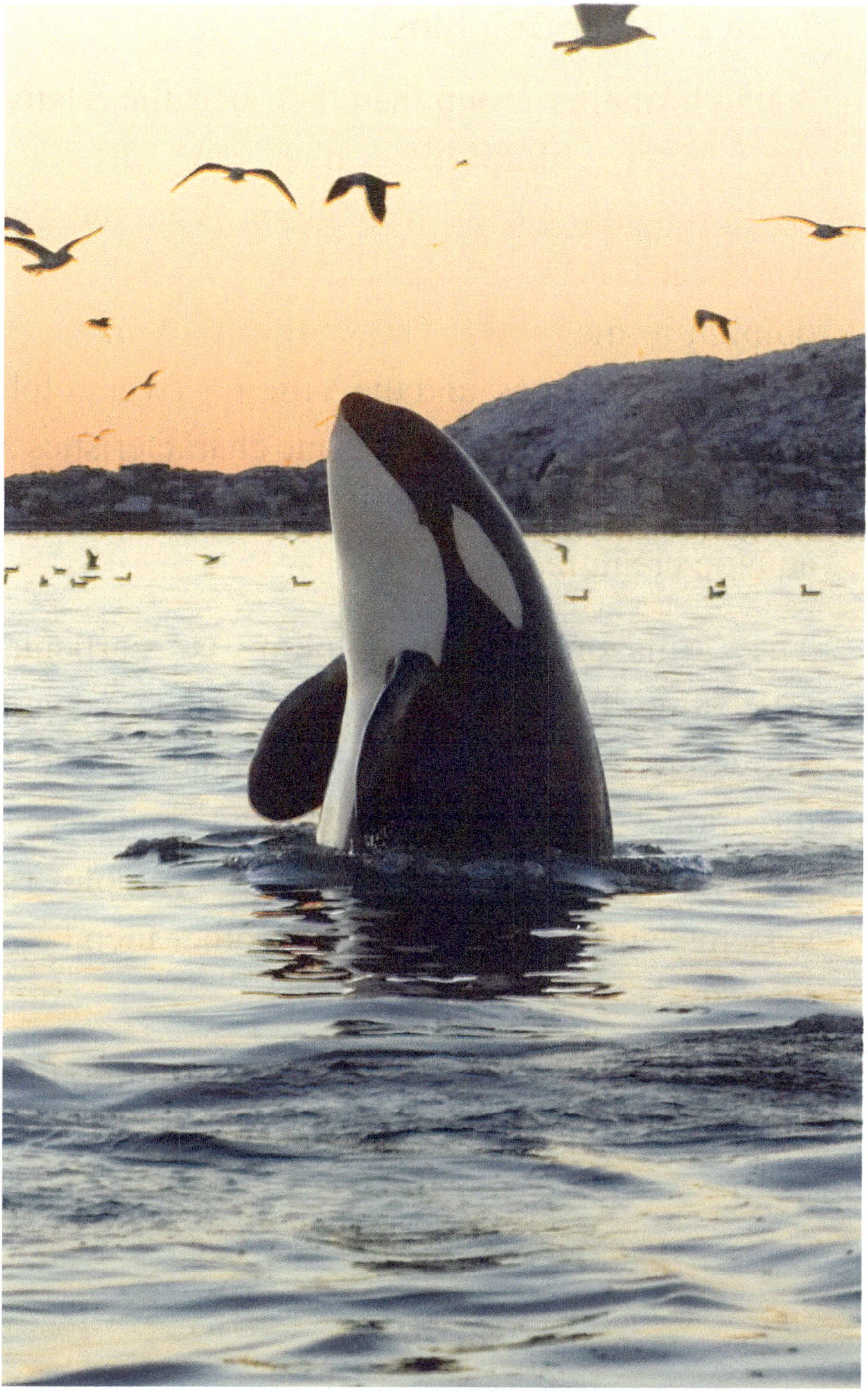

Type 2: River Dolphins

A much smaller group than their oceanic relatives, the **river dolphins** live in freshwater environments, mostly throughout Asia and South America. There are only five species of river dolphin in the world. The **Baiji**, the **Amazon**, the **Indus**, the **Ganges**, and the **Yangtze** river dolphin. Each species has its own unique characteristics and habitat, making them truly remarkable and special aquatic creatures.

The Amazon River dolphin is particularly interesting. It can turn its head a full 180 degrees, allowing it to scan its surroundings in all directions! This remarkable trait enhances its ability to spot prey, navigate through complex river systems, and communicate with other members of its pod.

You can see an Amazon River dolphin in the photograph on the next page.

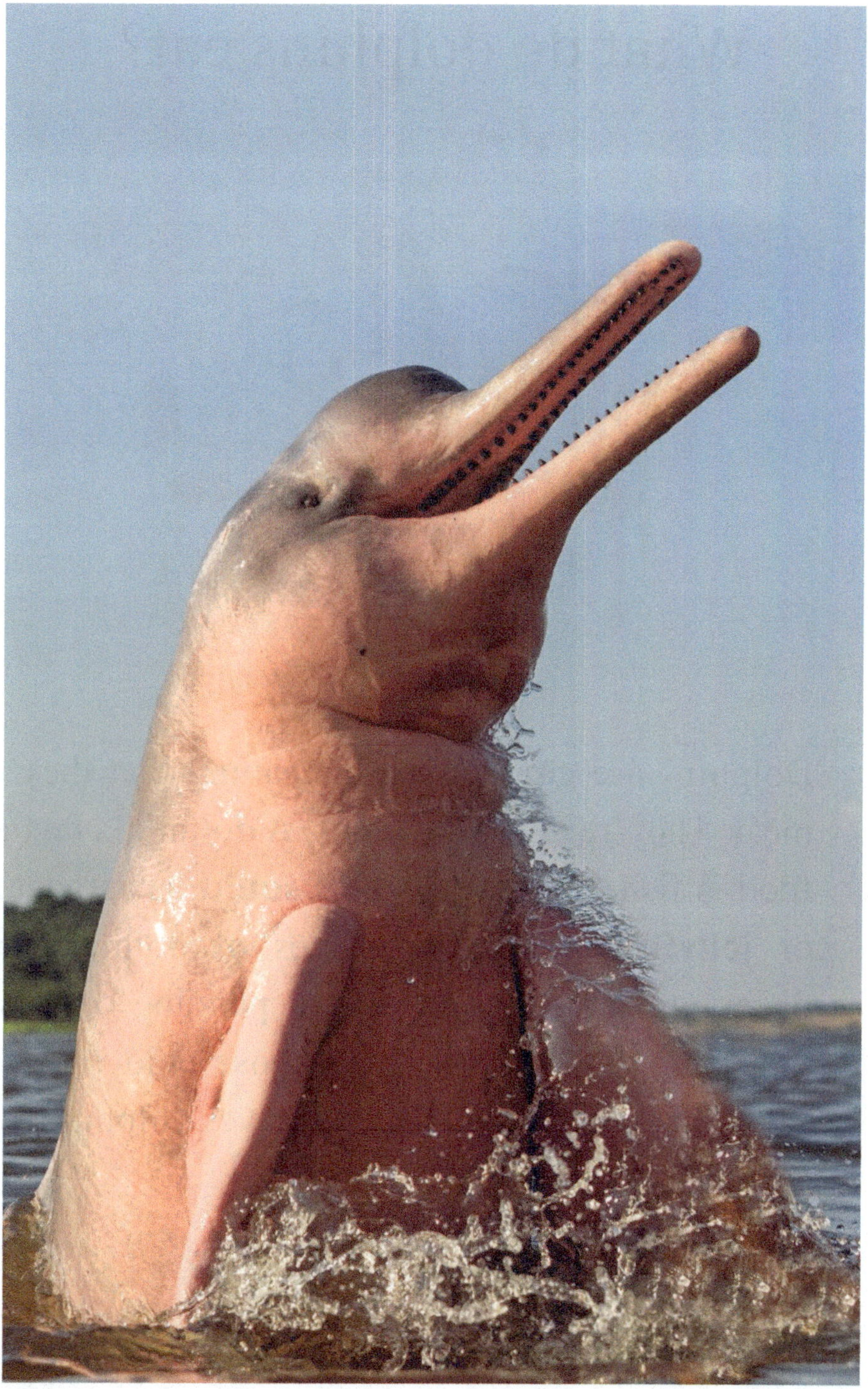

What do dolphins eat?

Dolphins are **carnivorous**, meaning that they eat meat. They're not vegetarians. A dolphin's favorite food is fish, but they also eat **squid**, **crustaceans**, or **jellyfish**. Different species of dolphin have different favorite delicacies, depending on where they live. The northern bottlenose enjoys a tasty salmon, whereas the Amazon River dolphin feasts on freshwater crabs.

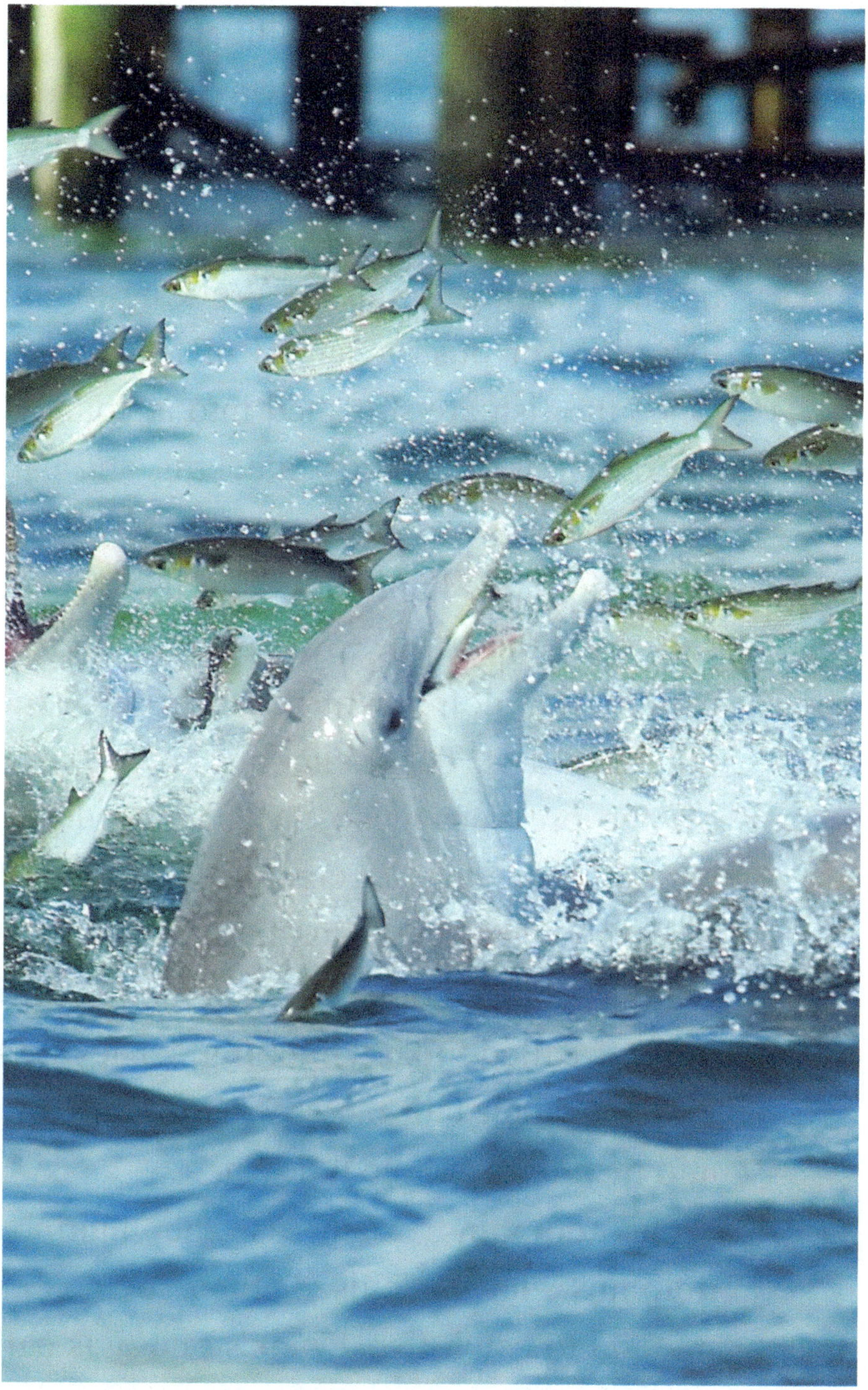

Because dolphins are so intelligent, they have developed a variety of creative ways to catch their food.

- Dolphins living in a large group (or "**pod**") use a "**herding**" strategy. Working together, they herd or push a school of fish together. Once the fish are squished into a small area, the dolphins take turns attacking and eating their captive prey.
- Some dolphins hunt alone and use a method called **echolocation** to help them find their prey. These dolphins make a series of high-pitched clicks. These clicking sounds bounce off the prey and echo back to the dolphin, allowing the clever creature to locate the whereabouts of the potential food.
- Other species of dolphins beat their prey in a process called **"fish whacking."** They hit the fish with their tail, thereby stunning the fish, and then they gobble it down.
- Some dolphins, such as the humpback dolphins, have devised their own crafty method to catch fish. Their strategy is called

bubble-net feeding. These dolphins blow a ring of bubbles around a school of fish, trapping them inside the ring. The dolphins then move in and help themselves to their dinner.

- Dolphins have also been known to use **tools** for hunting their prey. Bottlenose dolphins use sea sponges to help them dig for food on the ocean floor. This protects their beaks from getting scratched in the sea sand. Other dolphins make use of large shells to scoop up fish and swallow them, just like you or I would use a spoon!
- In some places, they even work with humans to earn their supper. When **fishermen** go out with their nets to catch massive quantities of fish, the dolphins tag along. They've learned to work with the fishermen because they know that if they stay close to them, then they may catch a few unsuspecting fish in the process.

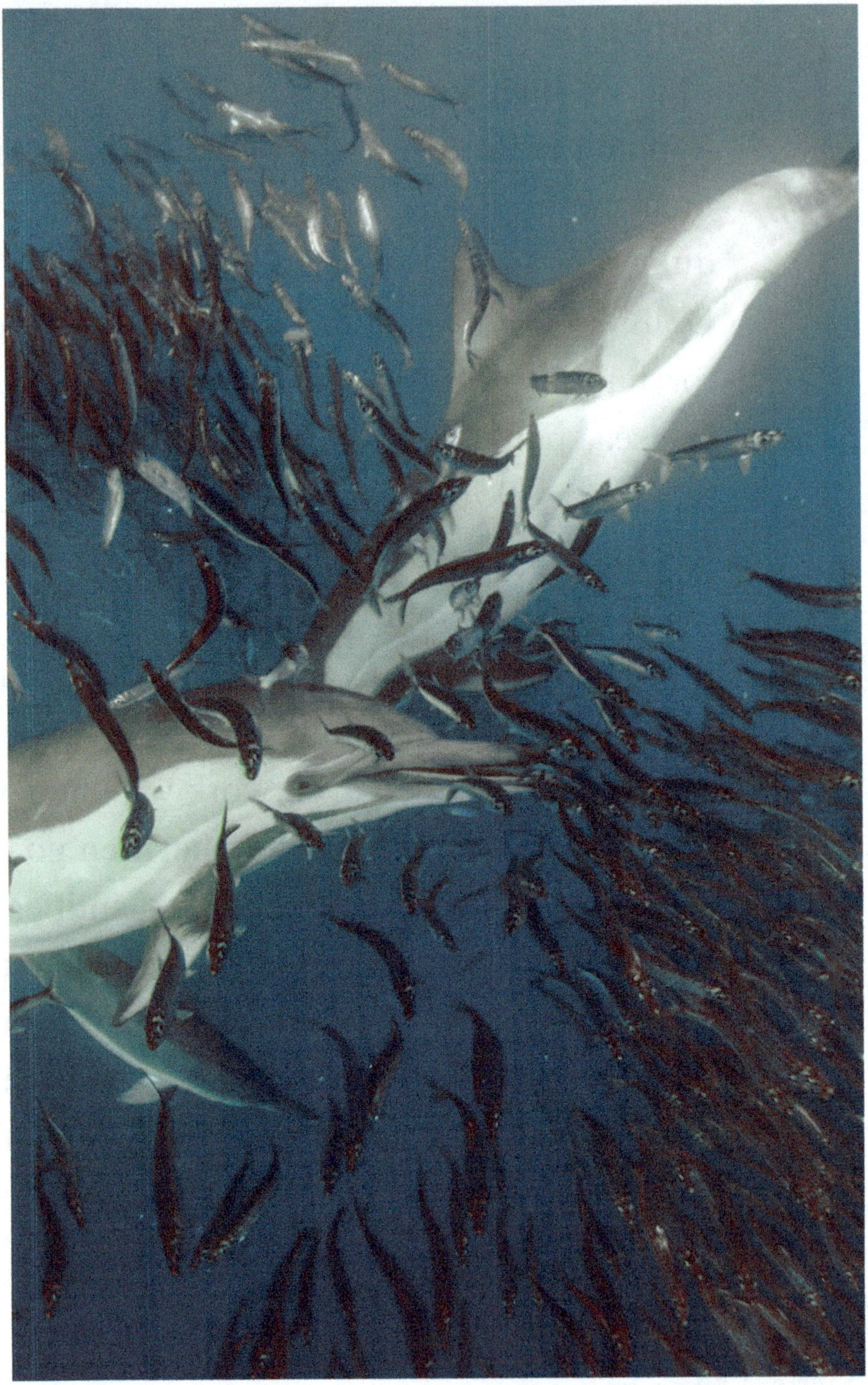

When the dolphins finally manage to catch their prey, it's time to eat it. But they don't chew like we do. Dolphins have somewhere between 100 and 200 teeth. Unlike us, they only have one set of teeth to last them an entire lifetime. We have two sets — our baby teeth and our adult teeth. Also, dolphins don't use their teeth for chewing. They use them to grasp and hang onto their prey before swallowing it whole! They even have three stomach chambers to digest it all. (Check out all the teeth in the mouth of the dolphin on the next page.)

What about water? What do they drink?

Well, dolphins don't need to drink water to stay alive. They receive all the hydration they need from the fish they consume. Fish are packed with water, and as dolphins consume them, they indirectly receive all the water they'll need. This clever adaptation allows dolphins to thrive in their marine environment without the need for fresh drinking water. Their bodies have evolved to efficiently extract the water from their prey, thus ensuring that they stay hydrated and healthy.

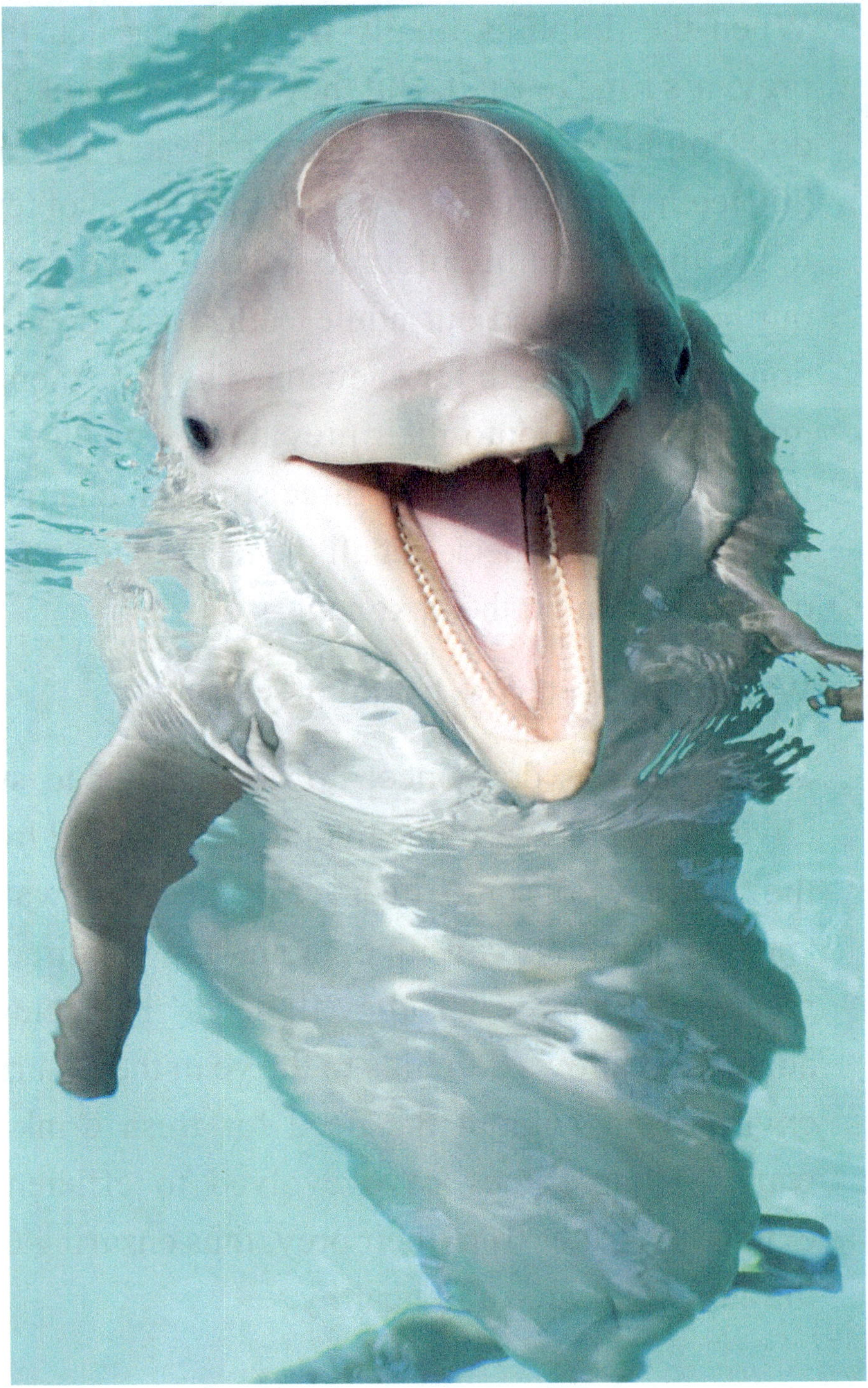

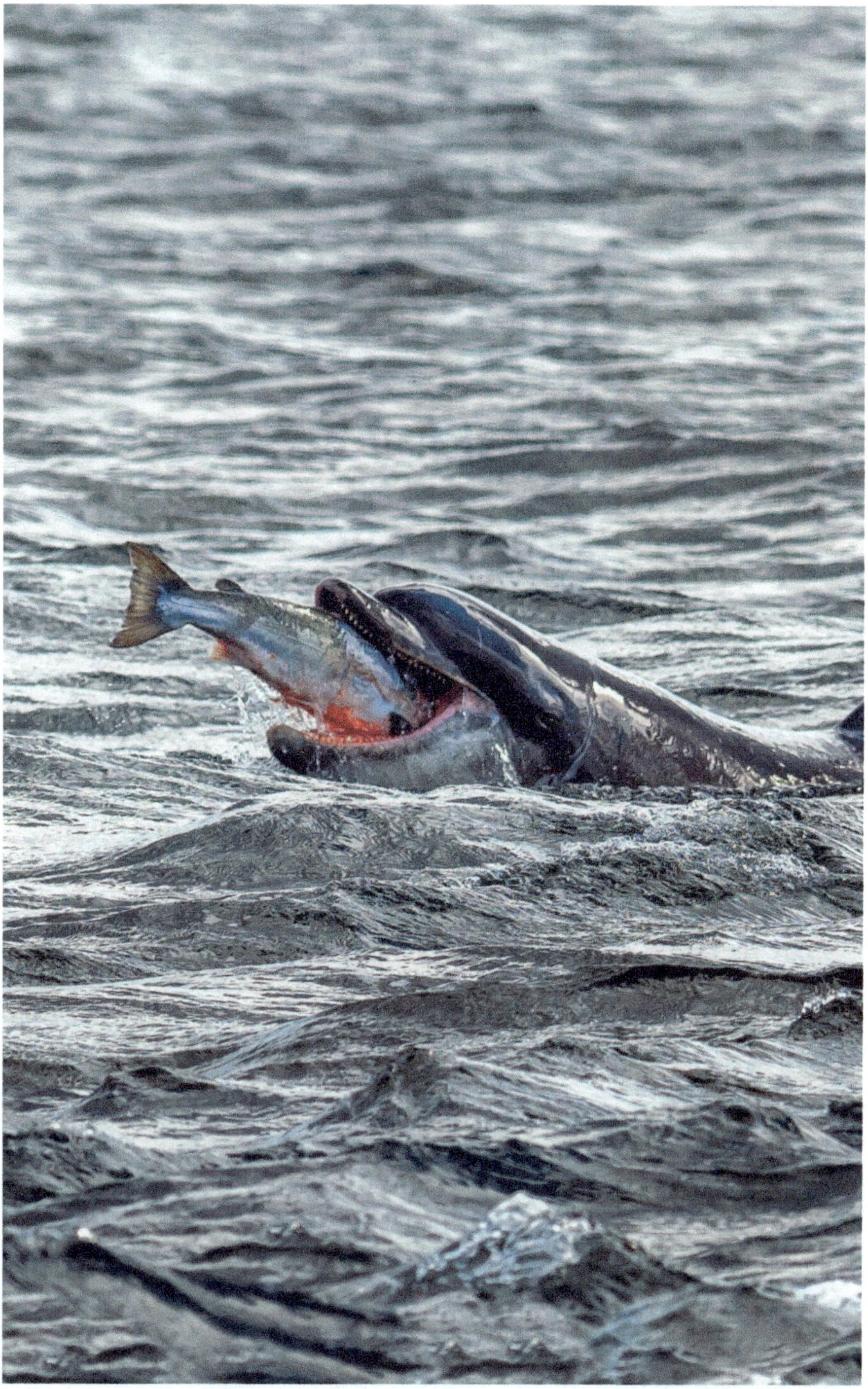

How do dolphins breathe?

Since dolphins are mammals, they must regularly come to the surface to breathe. If a dolphin can't reach the fresh air, it drowns. Because they spend their lives in the water, they have developed the ability to hold their breath for a long time, perhaps as long as 8 to 10 minutes. Some species of dolphins have special breathing techniques and are capable of staying underwater for up to 20 minutes!

Don't try that at home!

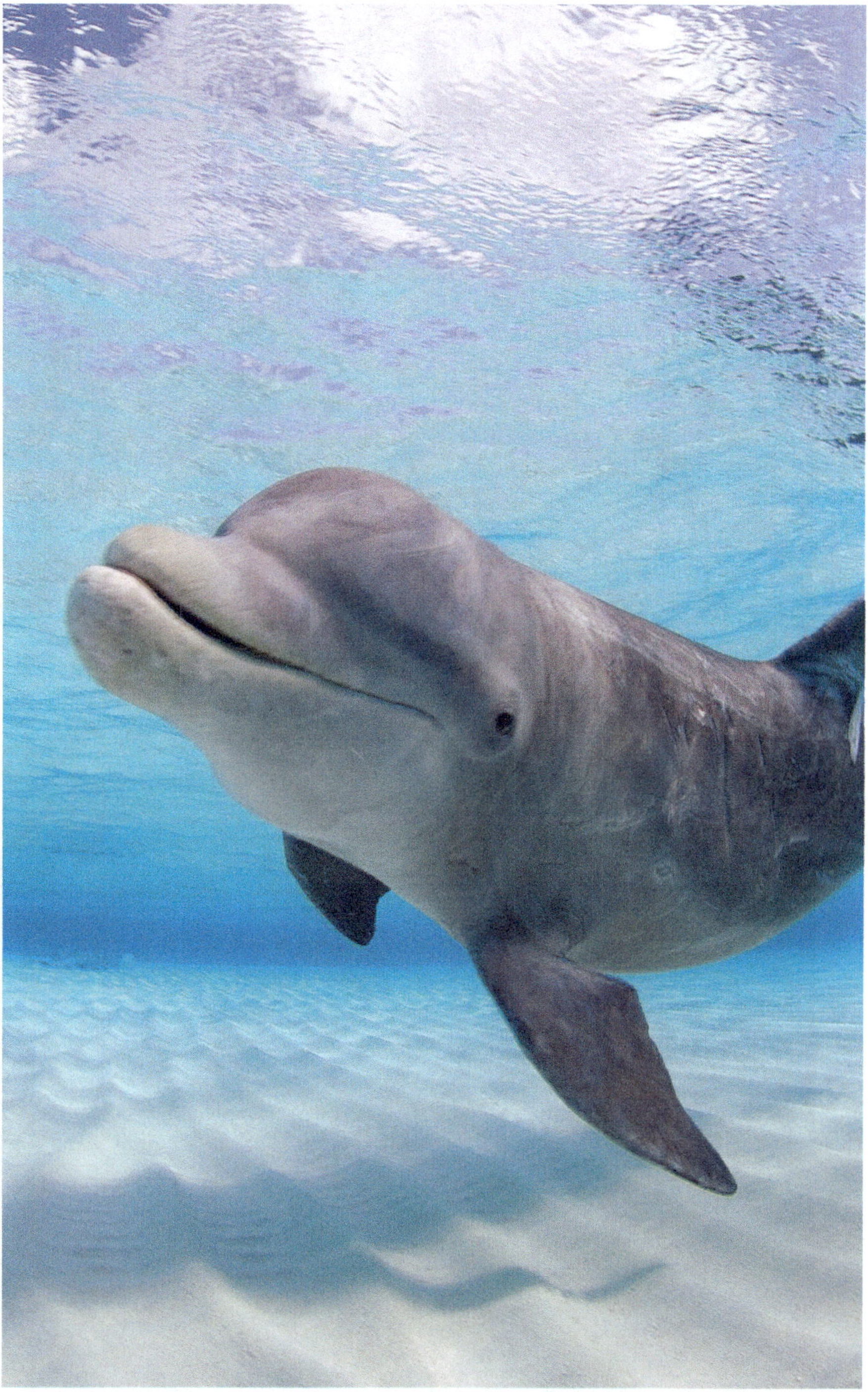

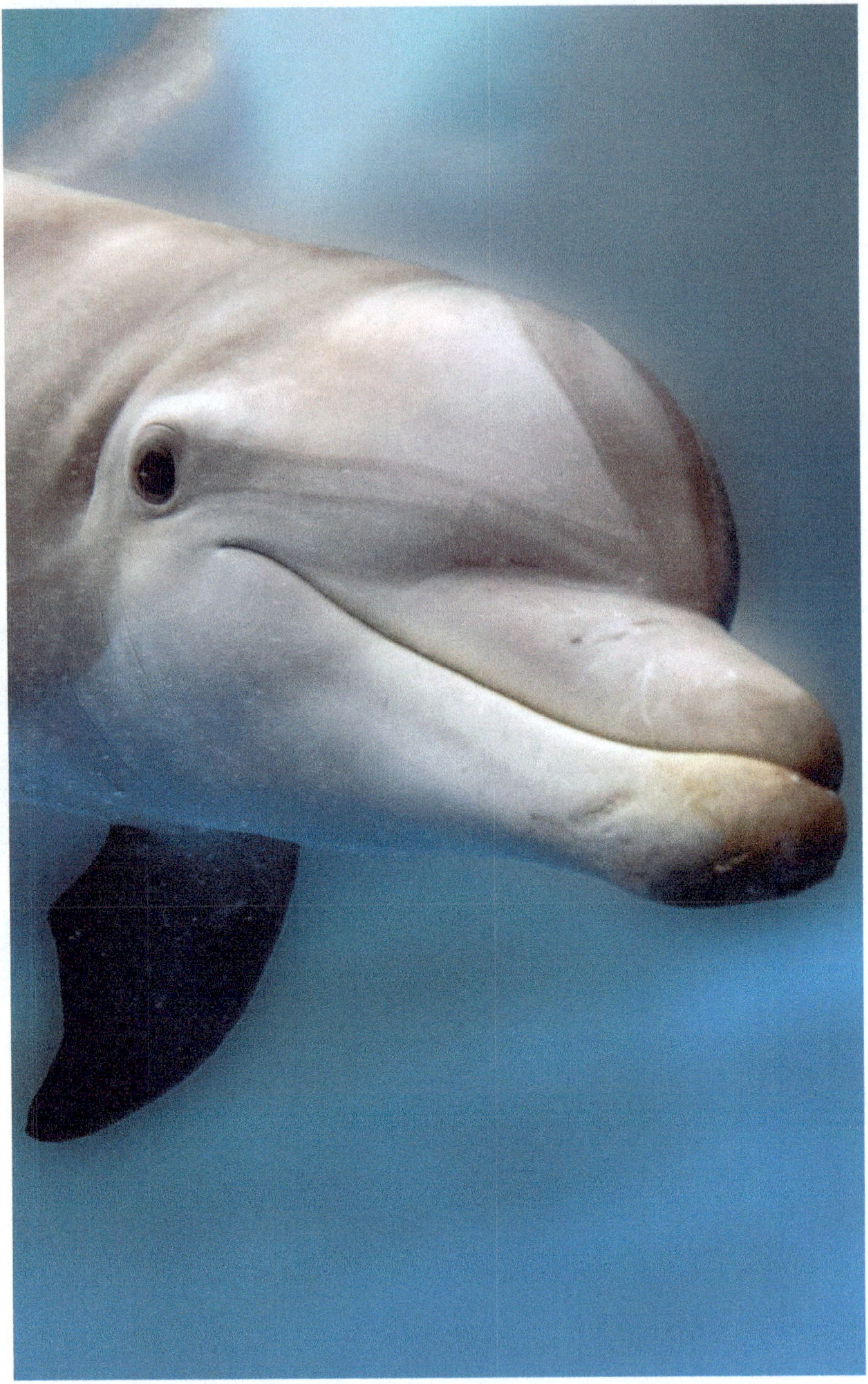

Remember when we mentioned the dolphin's "snout" earlier? You may be forgiven for thinking that dolphins breathe through it. In actuality, the snout is just for eating and not for breathing. Dolphins breathe through a single nostril located on top of their head called a "**blowhole**." This hole allows them to breathe without lifting much of their body out of the water.

As the dolphins surface, they blow used air out of their lungs and through the blowhole, squirting a fine spray of mist up into the air. Then they quickly take fresh air in through the blowhole again, before diving back under the water. To prevent water from getting in through the blowhole, they have a handy flap of muscle that covers the hole when they are underwater.

Notice the dolphin's blowhole in the next photograph.

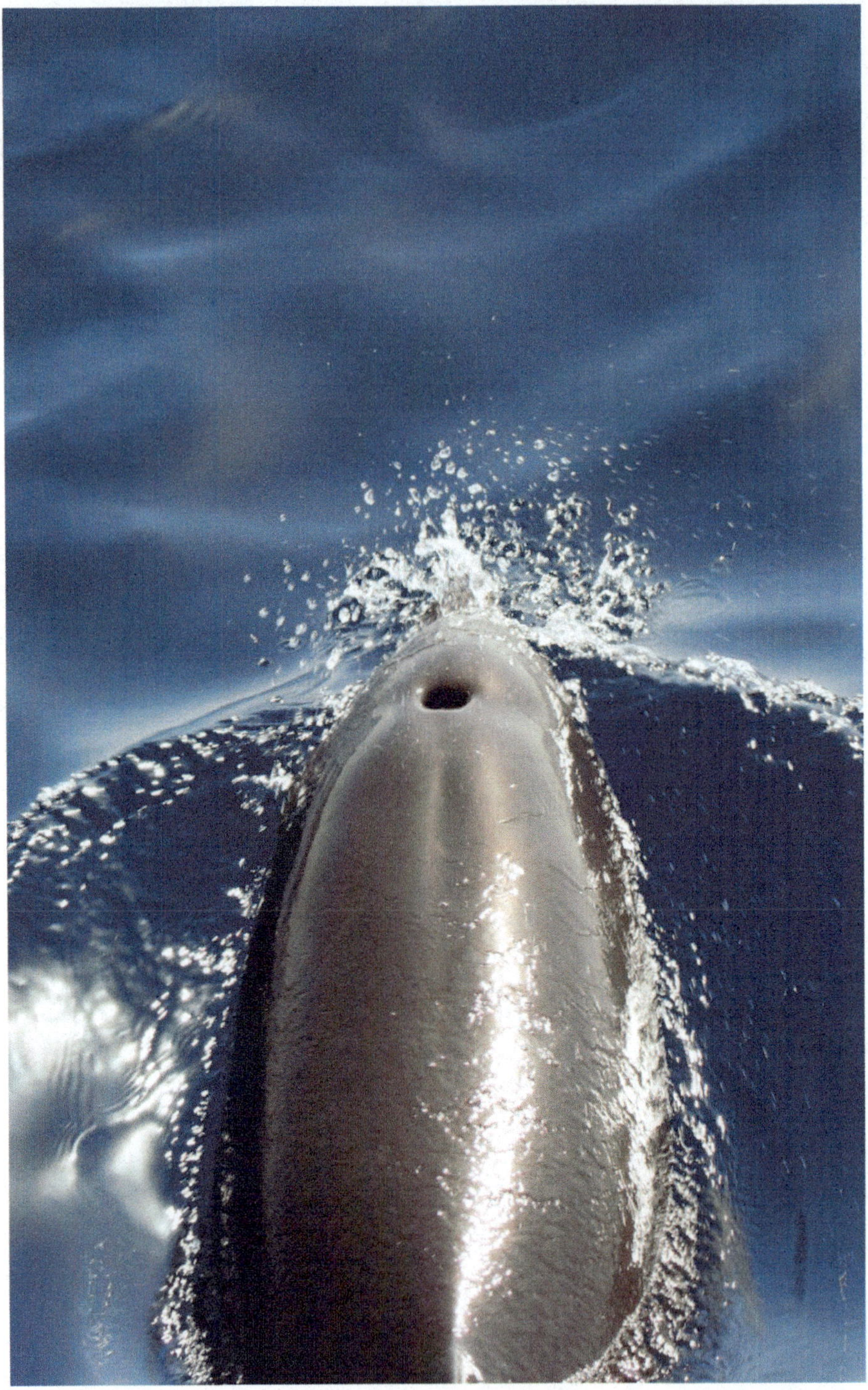

How do dolphins sleep?

Dolphins need to sleep to stay healthy, just like humans do. But you'll be fascinated to learn about the unusual way they sleep. You see, dolphins must be awake to breathe; they have to swim to the surface every few minutes to get air. But how do they sleep and swim at the same time?

Well, these brilliant creatures have developed a unique way of handling the problem.

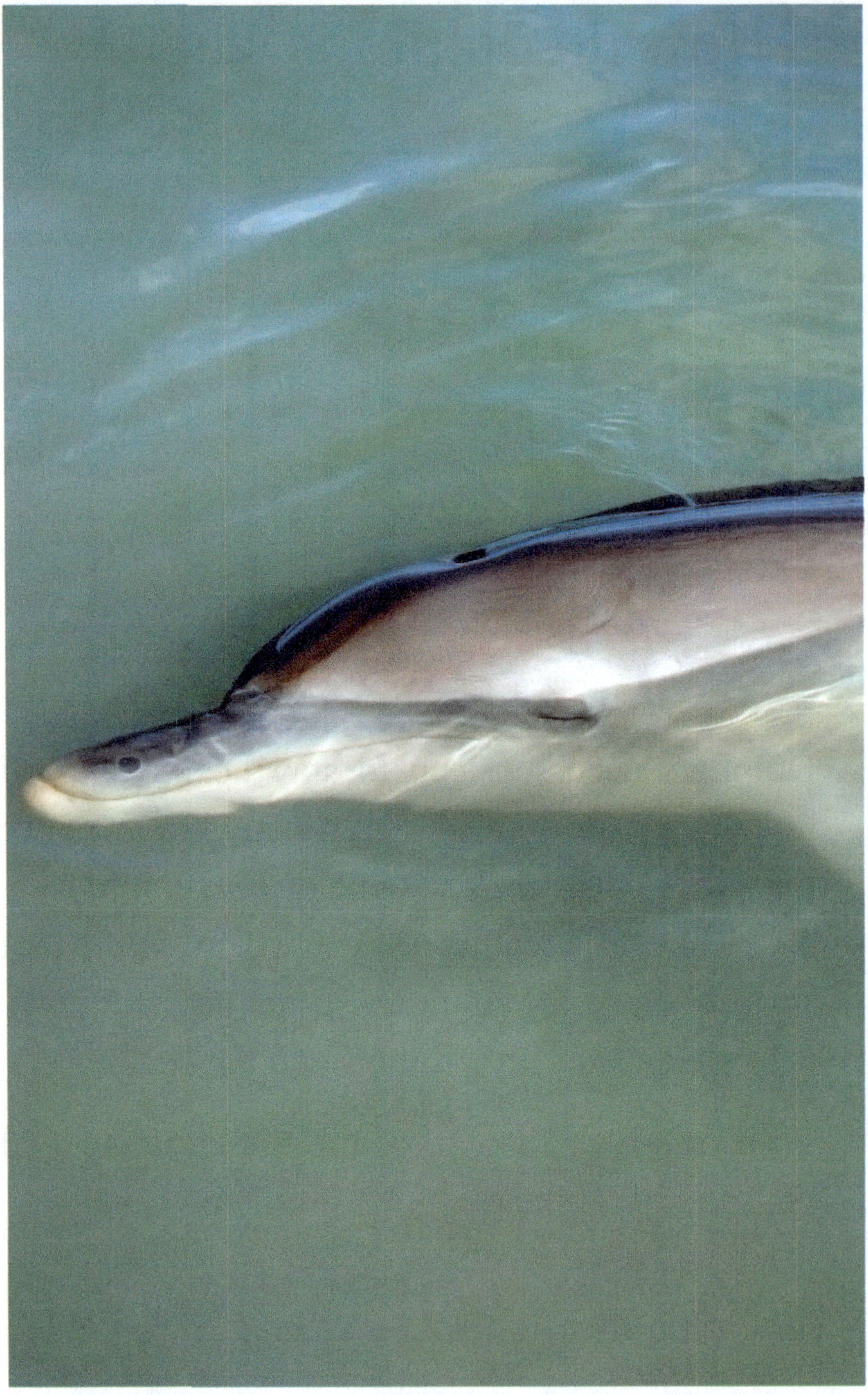

Dolphins don't take long snoozes. They take many short naps throughout the day, often of only a few minutes in length. Some dolphin species even sleep while swimming near the surface of the water, while other species rest on the ocean floor napping.

During their resting time, only one-half of the dolphin's brain sleeps! The other half is awake and on duty, taking control of the dolphin's swimming and breathing movements. This unique sleeping behavior is called **unihemispheric sleep**. It allows dolphins to maintain awareness of their surroundings while getting their necessary sleep time. This ensures that the dolphin will be ready to quickly respond to a potential threat, should one arise while it's slumbering.

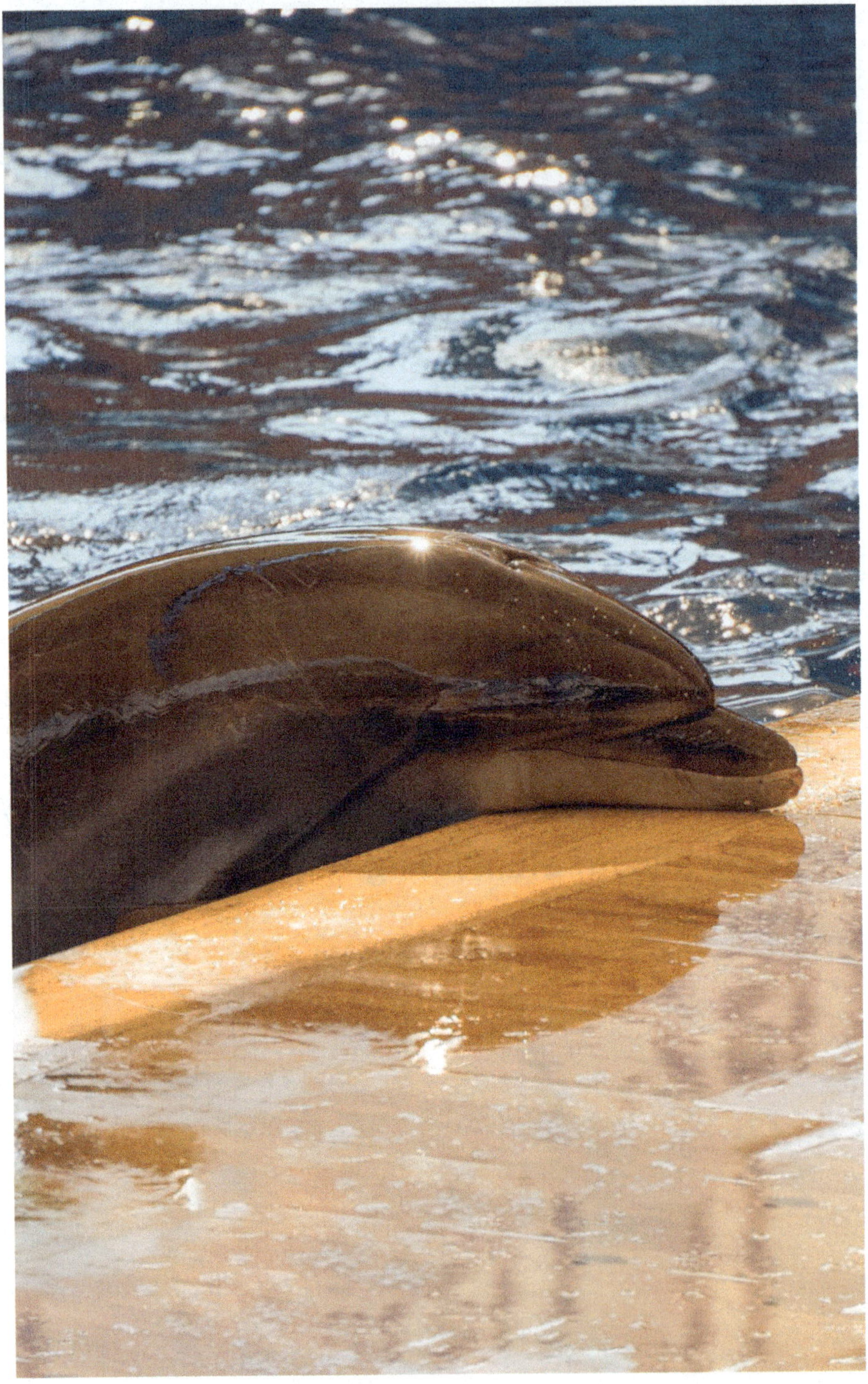

How do dolphins communicate?

Dolphins are extremely chatty creatures! They are so smart that they are able to "speak" to each other in their own secret dolphin language. They make clicks, squawks, squeaks, whistles, and yelps. Surprisingly, dolphins don't have vocal chords but create these noises through their blowholes. They also make use of body language, such as tail-slapping, head-butting, and even bubble-blowing.

Dolphins are very social animals. They love to interact with their dolphin family. They even enjoy interacting with us humans too! Dolphins live in a group known as a "**pod**." The members of the pod swim together, play together, hunt together, and protect each other from predators such as sharks.

Most pods range in size from only a few dolphins right up to 30 dolphins. Imagine all that chatting in such a large pod of dolphins! Sometimes, the dolphins hang out together to form a **super pod** where there may be hundreds of dolphins all swimming together like a big family!

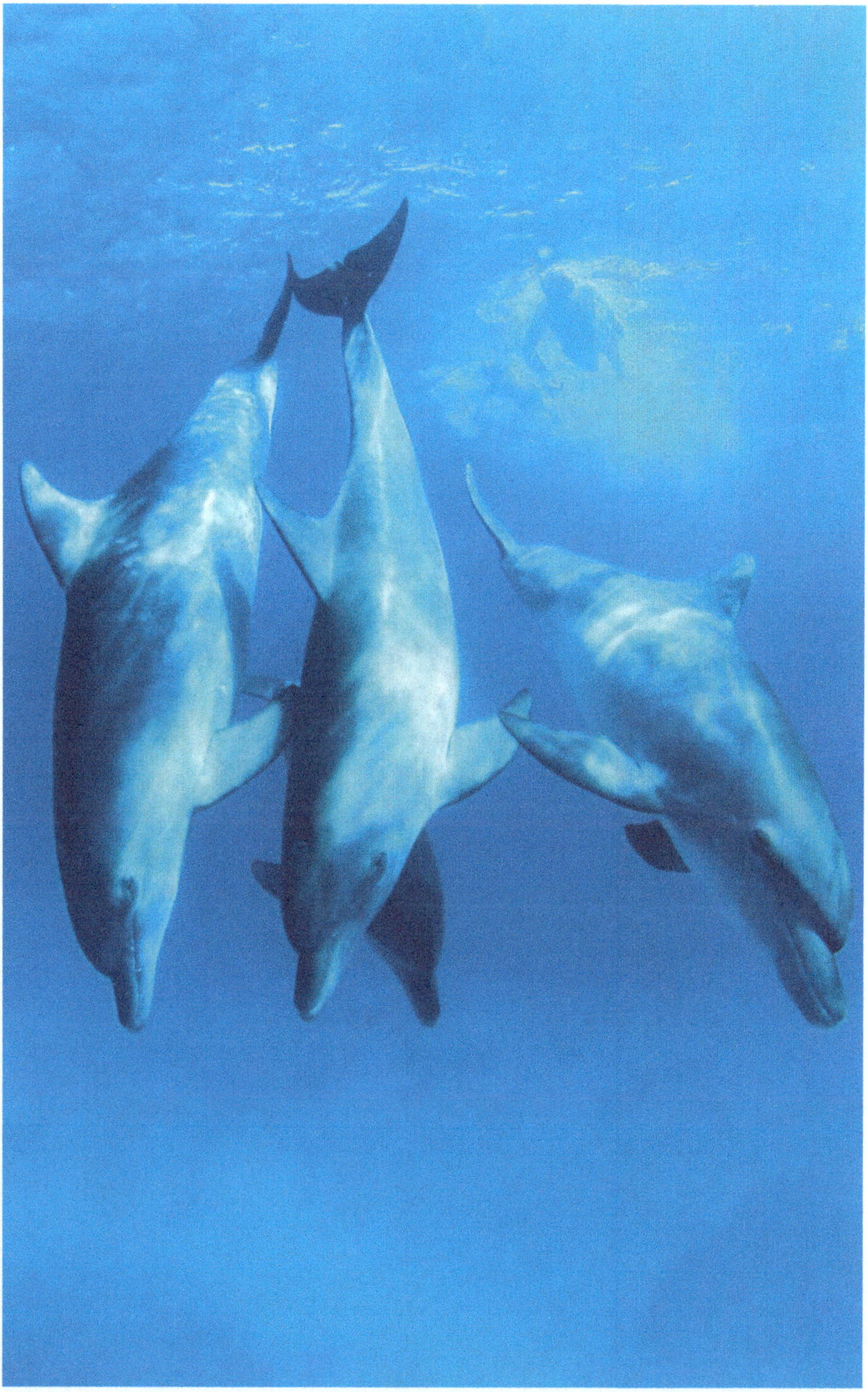

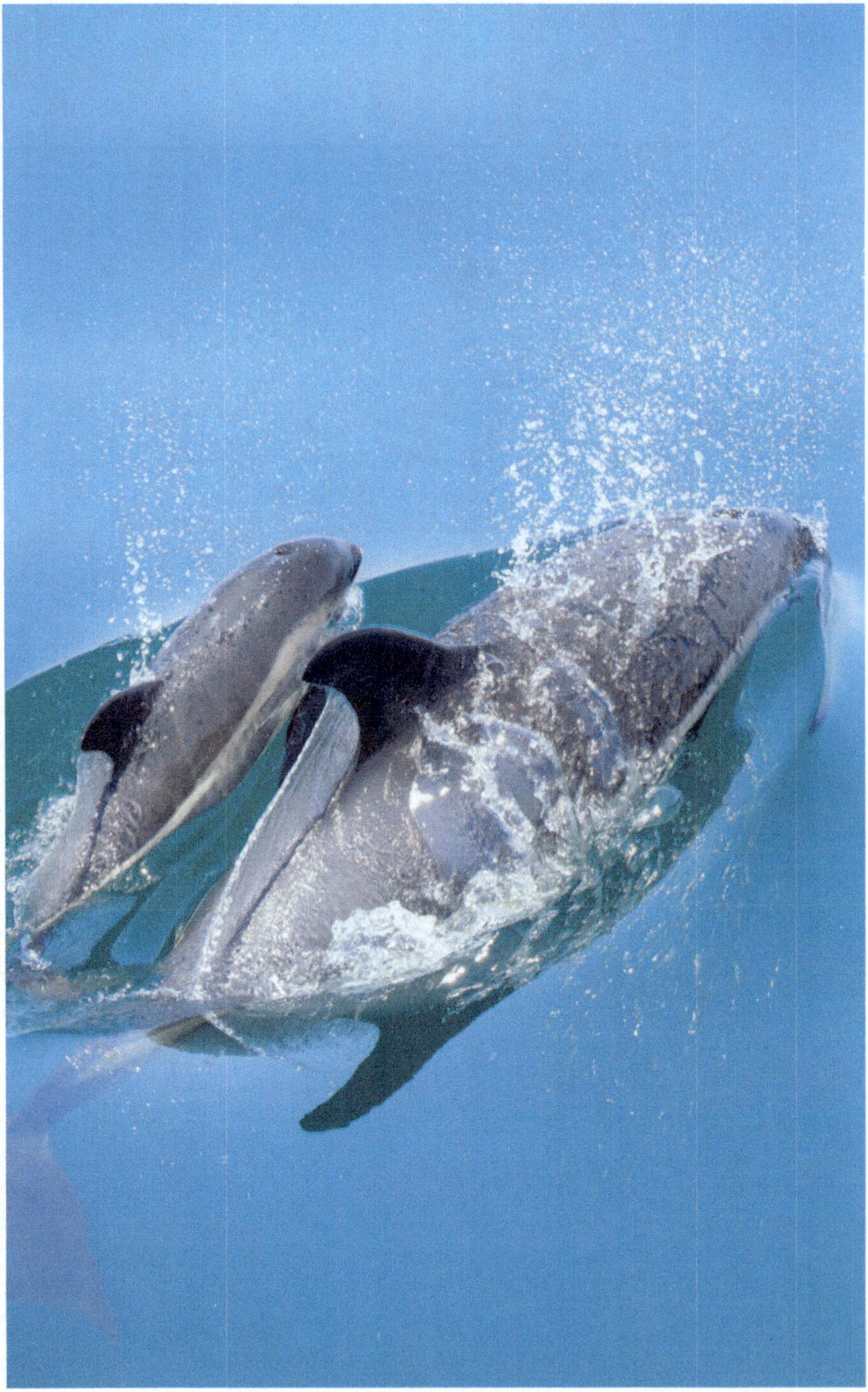

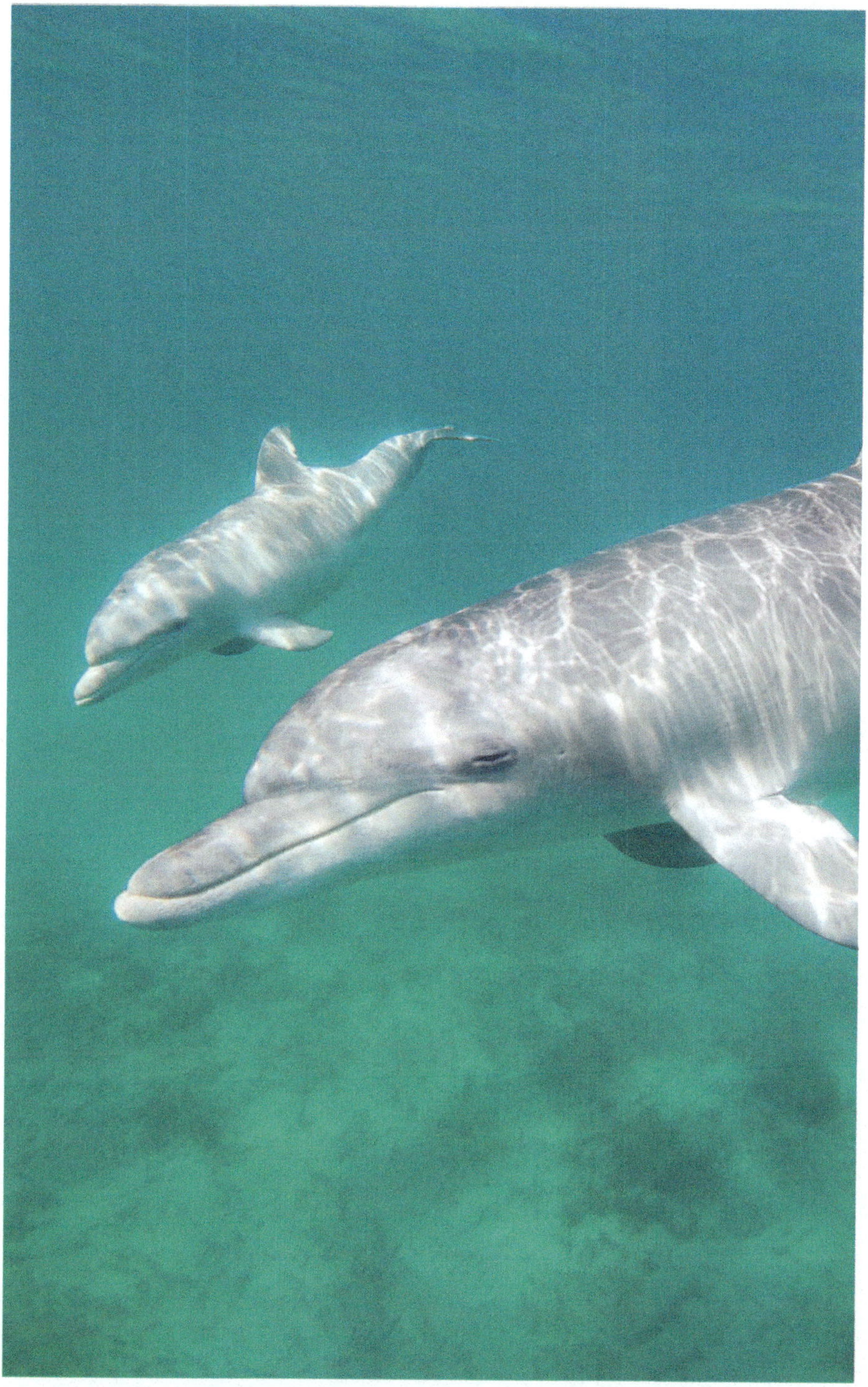

How fast can dolphins swim?

Dolphins are super-fast swimmers. The speed at which they swim depends on the species, age, and size. They have smooth, torpedo-shaped bodies which help them to glide effortlessly through the water. On either side of their bodies, they have pointed flippers or fins, and they have a triangular fin on their back.

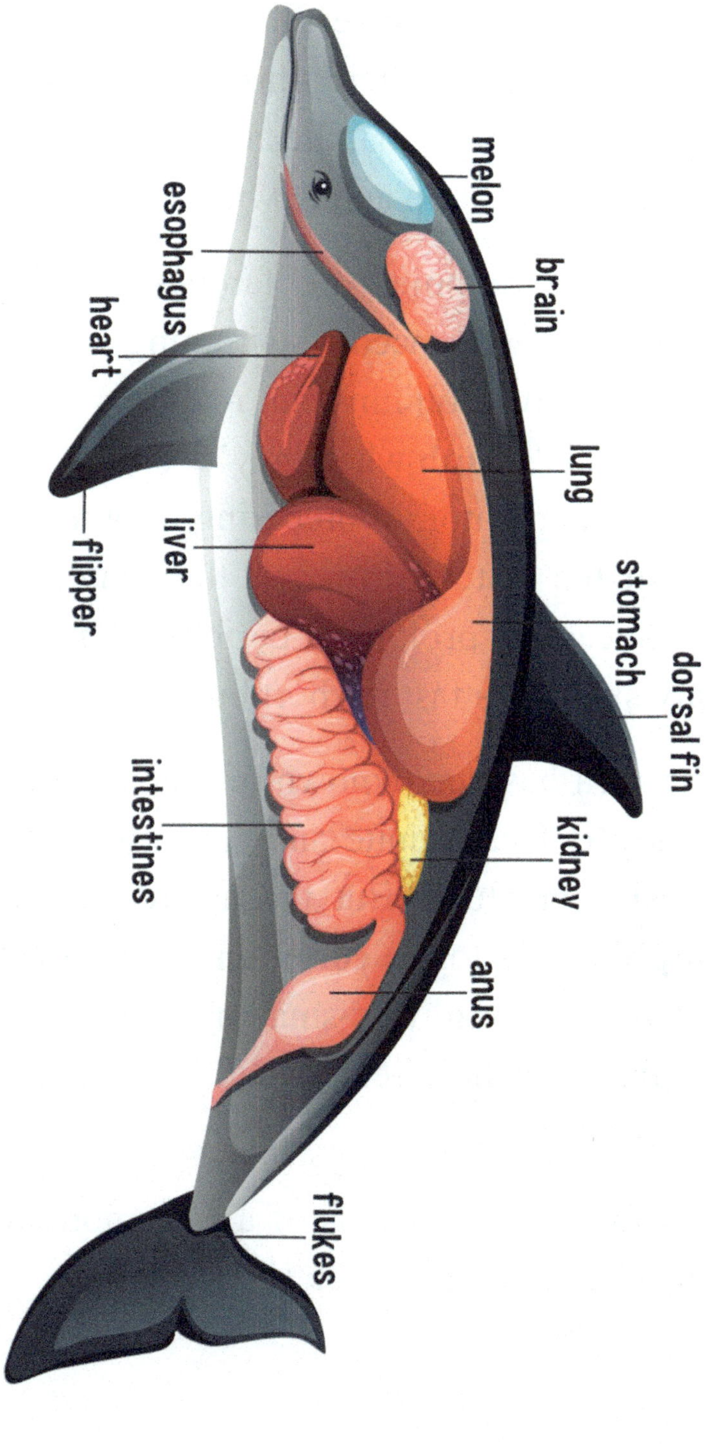
melon
brain
esophagus
heart
lung
liver
flipper
stomach
dorsal fin
intestines
kidney
anus
flukes

Dolphins have a powerful tail that moves up and down to propel them through the water. (It's interesting to note that the tail of a fish moves from side to side, not up and down.)

Bottlenose dolphins are famous for their water acrobatics and speedy swimming skills. If they need to, most dolphins can regularly reach speeds of around **22 mph** when they're chasing their prey, fleeing a predator, or preparing for a massive jump out of the water. However, they cannot maintain this speed for prolonged periods, and they tend to only swim this fast in short bursts.

The orca has been known to reach a top speed of **34 mph**. That's quite an achievement for such a massive creature! But the award for the **fastest dolphin** goes to the **common dolphin** *(Delphinus delphis)*. This guy is smaller than the bottlenose dolphin, but he's really fast; he can go **37 mph** when sprinting.

The following photo is of a Common Dolphin in Gibraltar. See how sleek he is?

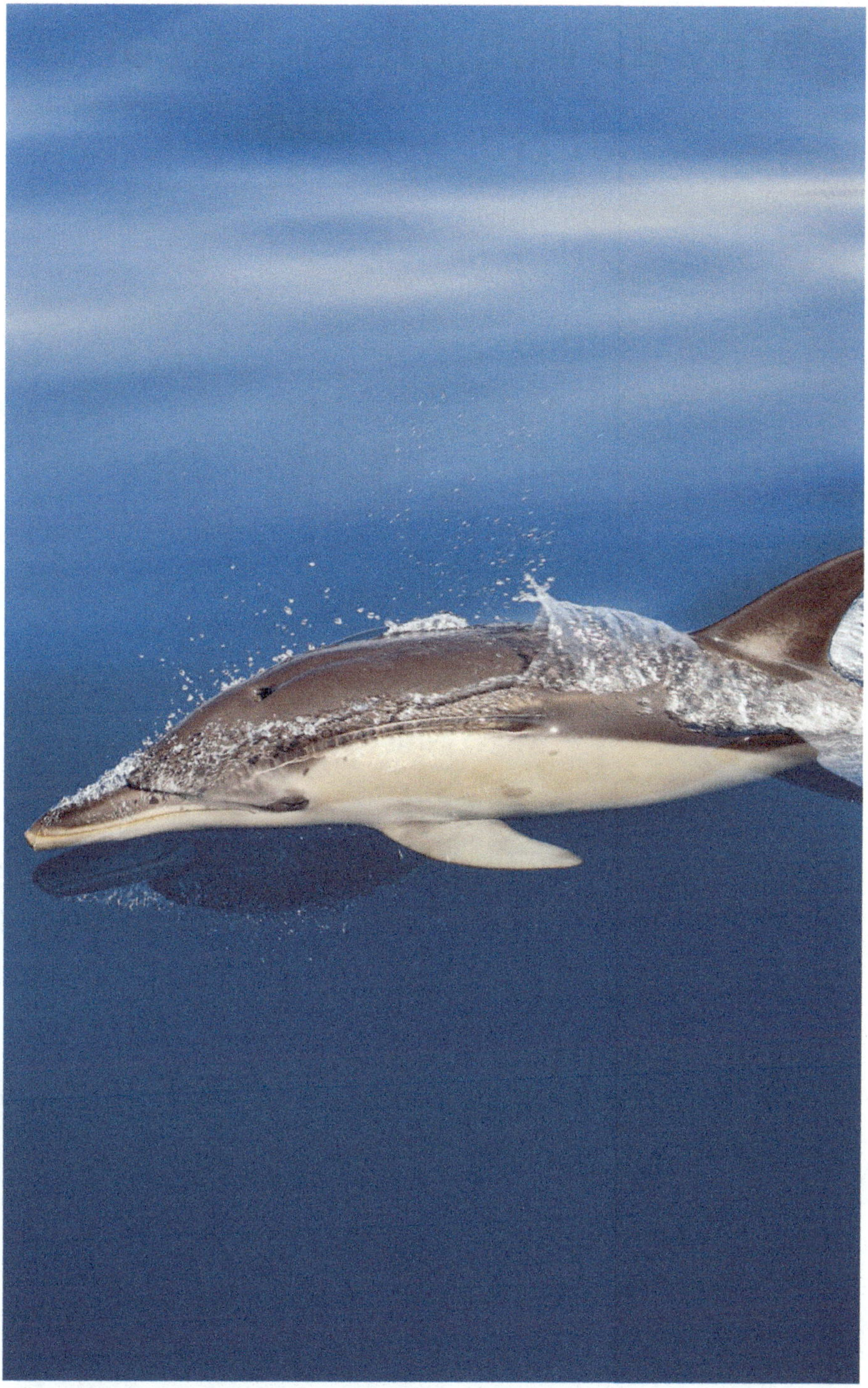

Why do dolphins jump out of the water?

You've probably seen a dolphin jump out of the sea before. They're pretty famous for leaping out of the water, doing flips, and splashing into the waves. These dolphin leaps have a special name; they're called **"breaching."** Some dolphins can launch themselves as much as 20 feet out of the air!

But have you ever wondered why they do this?

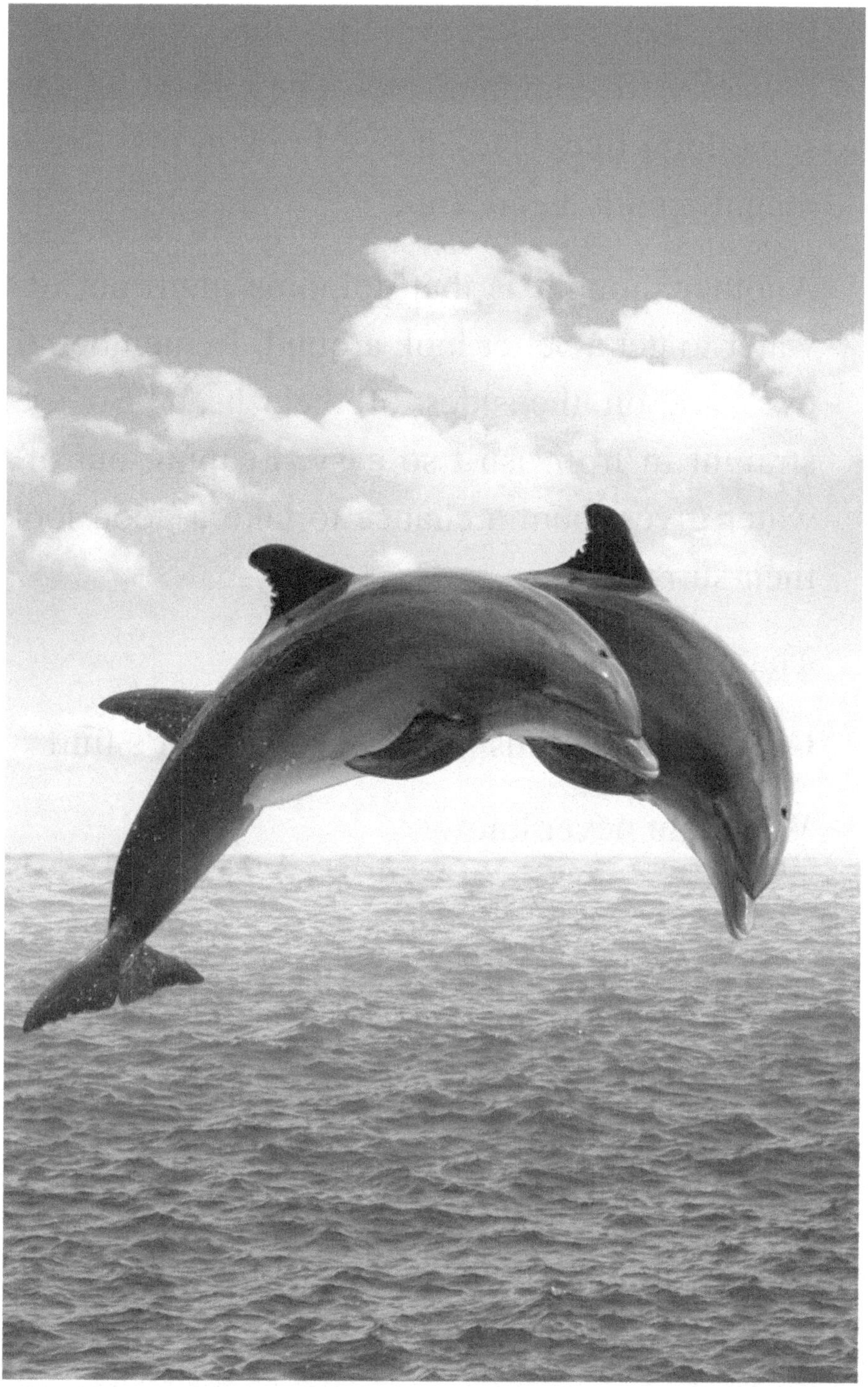

Some scientists believe that this is a way for dolphins to communicate. They may be saying something like, "Hey there! Look at me. See how magnificently I can leap!"

Another thought is that dolphins jump out of the water to get a better look around. Remember, their eyes are on the sides of their head. So seeing straight in front isn't so easy. Leaping out of the water gives them a chance to take a good look at their surroundings.

That might be the reason.

Or maybe dolphins just leap because it's fun!

We might never know…

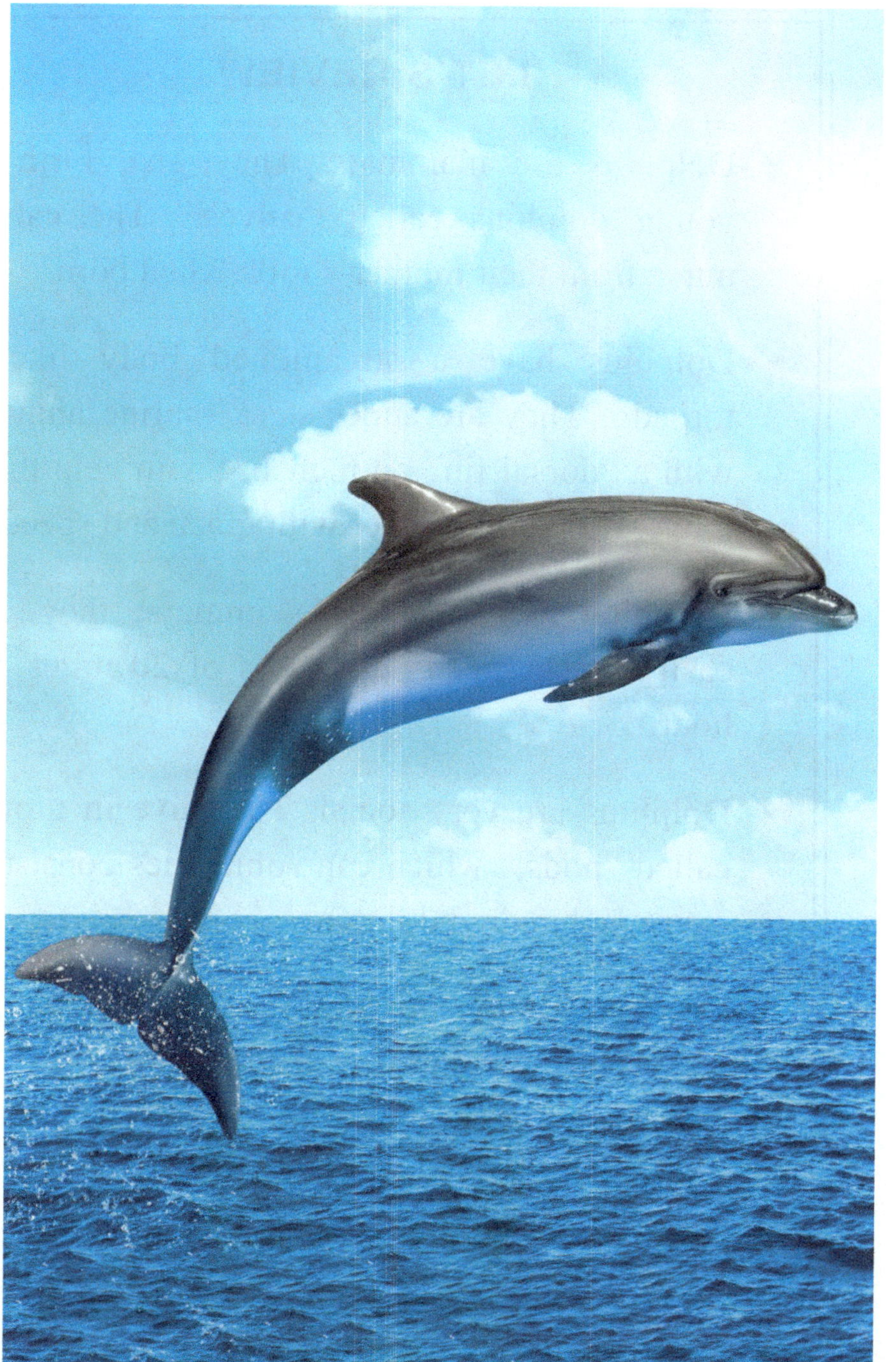

LET'S REVIEW

- ✓ Dolphins are mammals. They give birth to young dolphins called "calves." The calves nurse from their mother's milk when born.

- ✓ Dolphins have a streamlined body like a torpedo. They are super sleek marine animals with a "dorsal fin" on their backs to help them move through the water with grace and speed.

- ✓ Dolphins are excellent swimmers; they can easily reach speeds in excess of 20 miles per hour.

- ✓ Dolphins are very social. They live in groups called "pods," which can sometimes consist of over one hundred dolphins.

- ✓ Dolphins have a special organ called a "melon" on their forehead. They use it for "echolocation." The echoes help them to navigate through the ocean.

How intelligent are dolphins?

Did you know that the world's oceans contain some of the smartest animals on the planet? Dolphins and whales might be called the "Einsteins of the sea."

Dolphins are well known for their intelligence.

But just how smart are they?

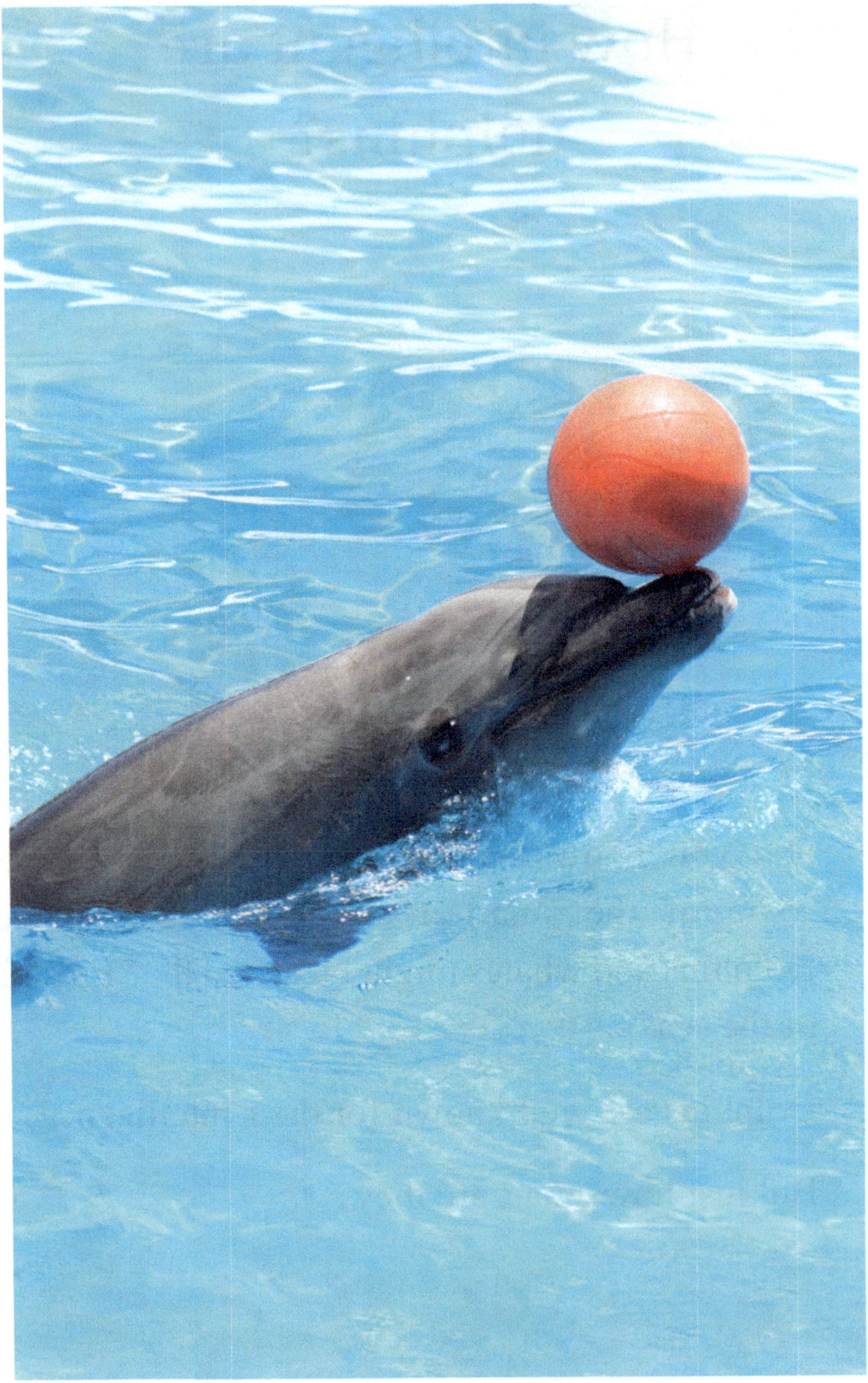

Well, the brain of a dolphin is actually larger than a human brain. It weighs a whopping 3.5 pounds! That's a lot of brain…

A human brain only weighs about 3 pounds. But remember, dolphins have a larger body than we do. Scientists use a scale called the **brain-to-body weight ratio** to estimate intelligence. They compare the weight of the brain to the weight of the entire body. The higher the weight of the brain compared to the body, the more intelligent the animal might be.

Based on this calculation, dolphins are the second smartest animals on earth after humans. We think they're even smarter than chimpanzees and apes — who are famous for being pretty brainy.

This remarkable intelligence allows the dolphins to solve puzzles and learn tricks with remarkable ease. Researchers have even used dolphins to help find lost objects in the sea.

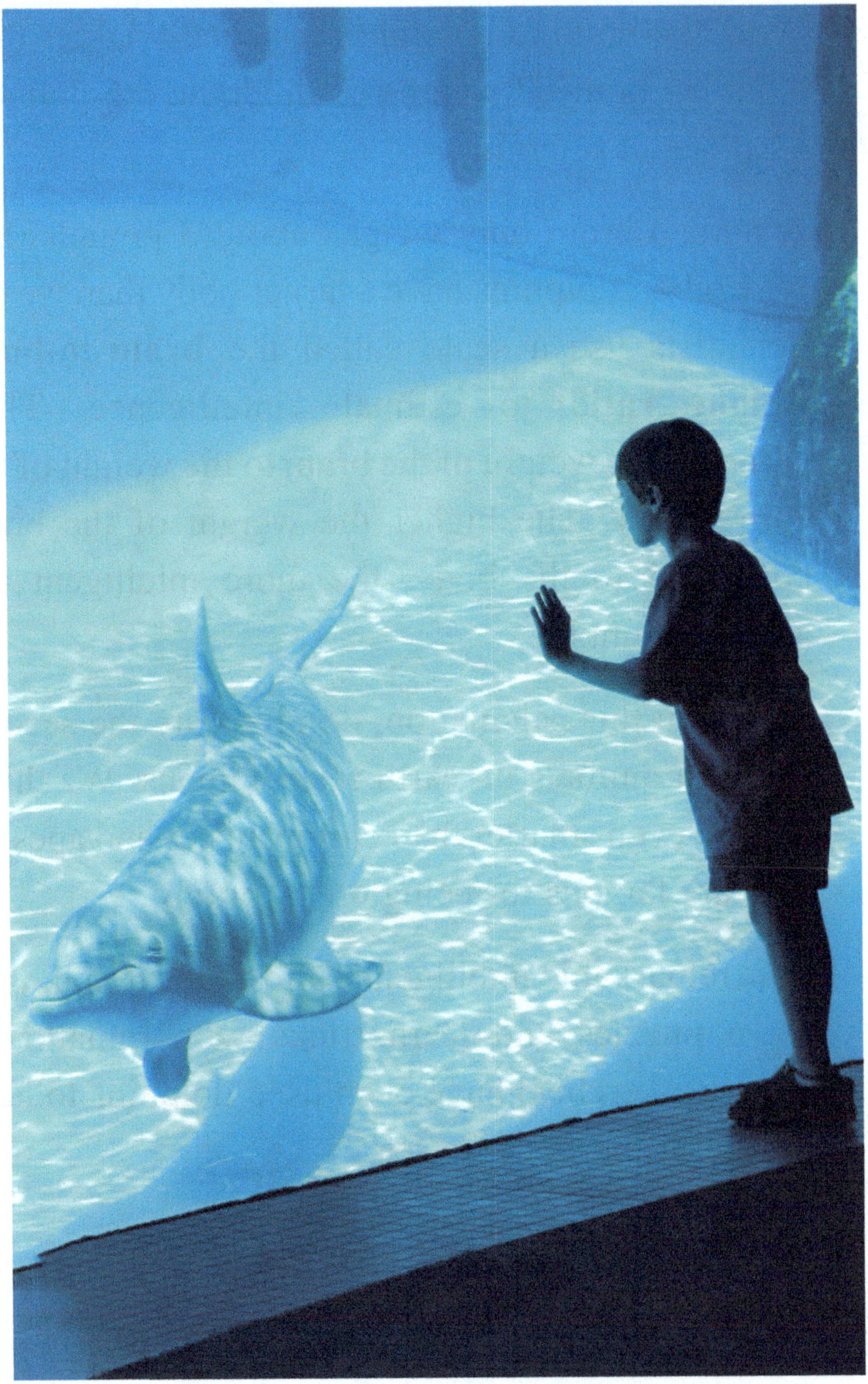

Also, dolphins are one of the few animals that are able to recognize themselves in a mirror. This is a skill that most animals do not have. Other than humans, only the **bottlenose dolphin**, **elephants**, **chimps**, and **magpie** birds are able to recognize their own reflection. Interestingly, dolphins can do this by the age of only seven months old. (It takes human children twelve months to do.)

When scientists put mirrors in dolphin tanks, the dolphins like to inspect the parts of their bodies that they usually can't get a good look at. They also like to open their mouths and examine their teeth. Sometimes they dance and twirl in front of the mirror too — maybe just to see how cute they can be!

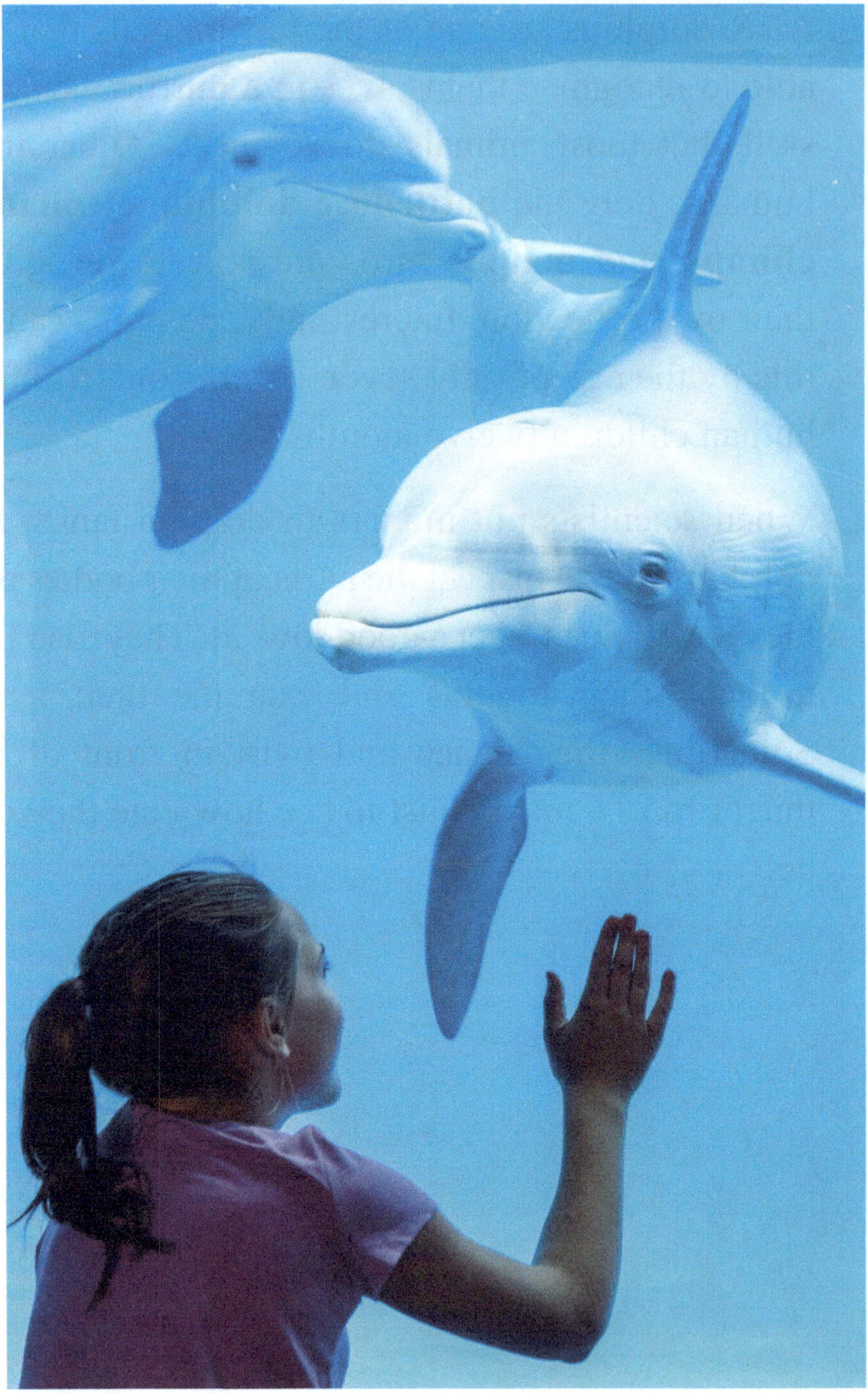

How long do dolphins live?

A dolphin's lifespan depends on a number of factors, including the species in question, its diet, current health status, and habitat. Their favorite food may not always be available to them. Or they may be exposed to pollutants in their preferred swimming area. All of these factors affect the lifespan of a dolphin, and any marine animal in the area.

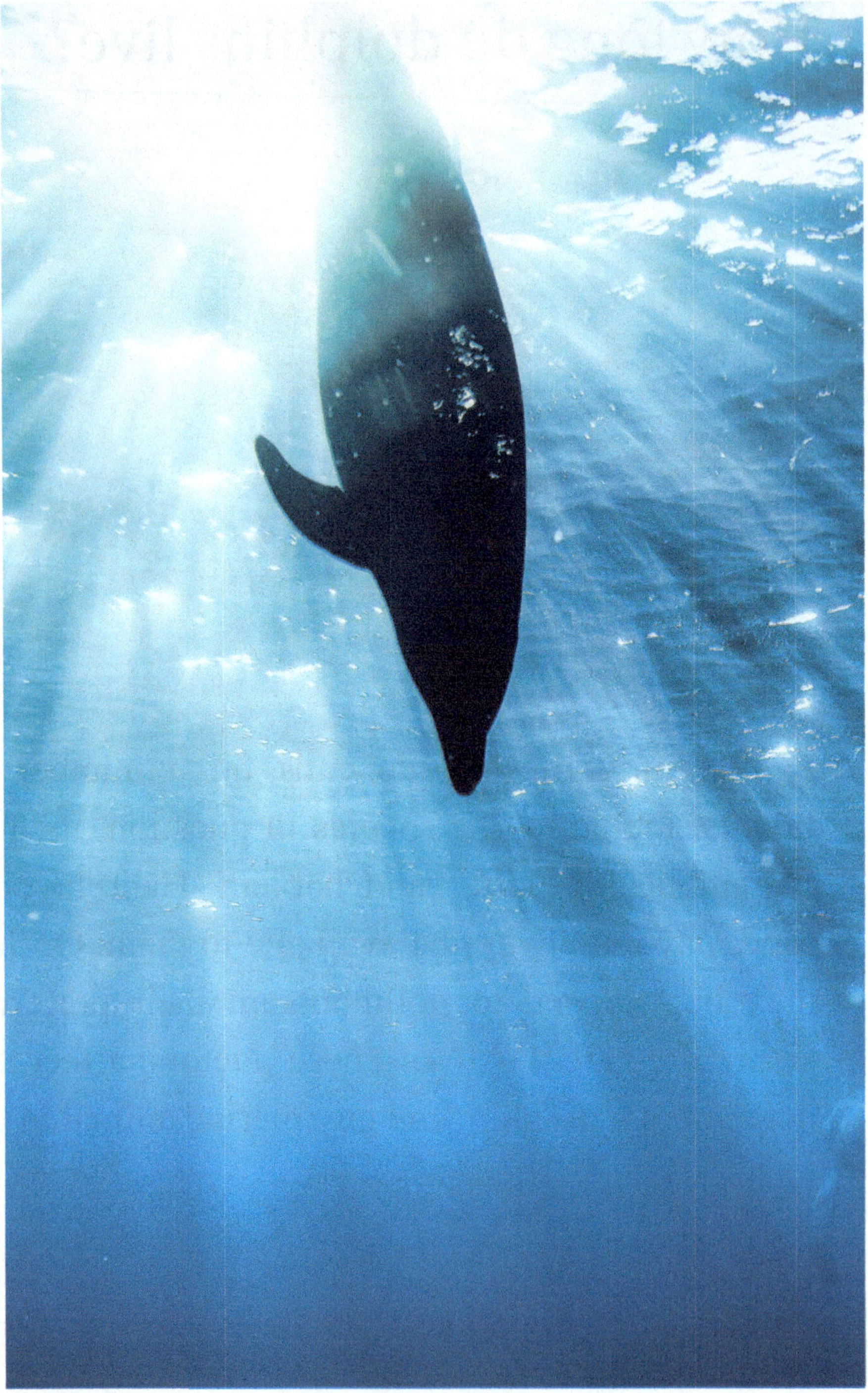

Perhaps the most crucial variable that determines a dolphin's lifespan is the state of its habitat. Some dolphins live in the wild, but many live in captivity — such as in aquariums or waterparks. Generally, dolphins living in captivity have a shorter lifespan than those living in the wild.

- **Bottlenose dolphins** in the wild can live for up to 50 years. But, in captivity, they only live for 25.
- Wild female **orcas** have been known to live for a staggering 90 years, though the average lifespan for a female orca is between 50 to 80. But in captivity, orcas only live for around 13 years.

These are very distressing numbers.

We're not really sure why the lives of dolphins in captivity are so short. But scientists and conservationists have discovered that dolphins kept in captivity seem to experience stress. They become depressed when they're separated from their family members and when they have limited interaction with other dolphins.

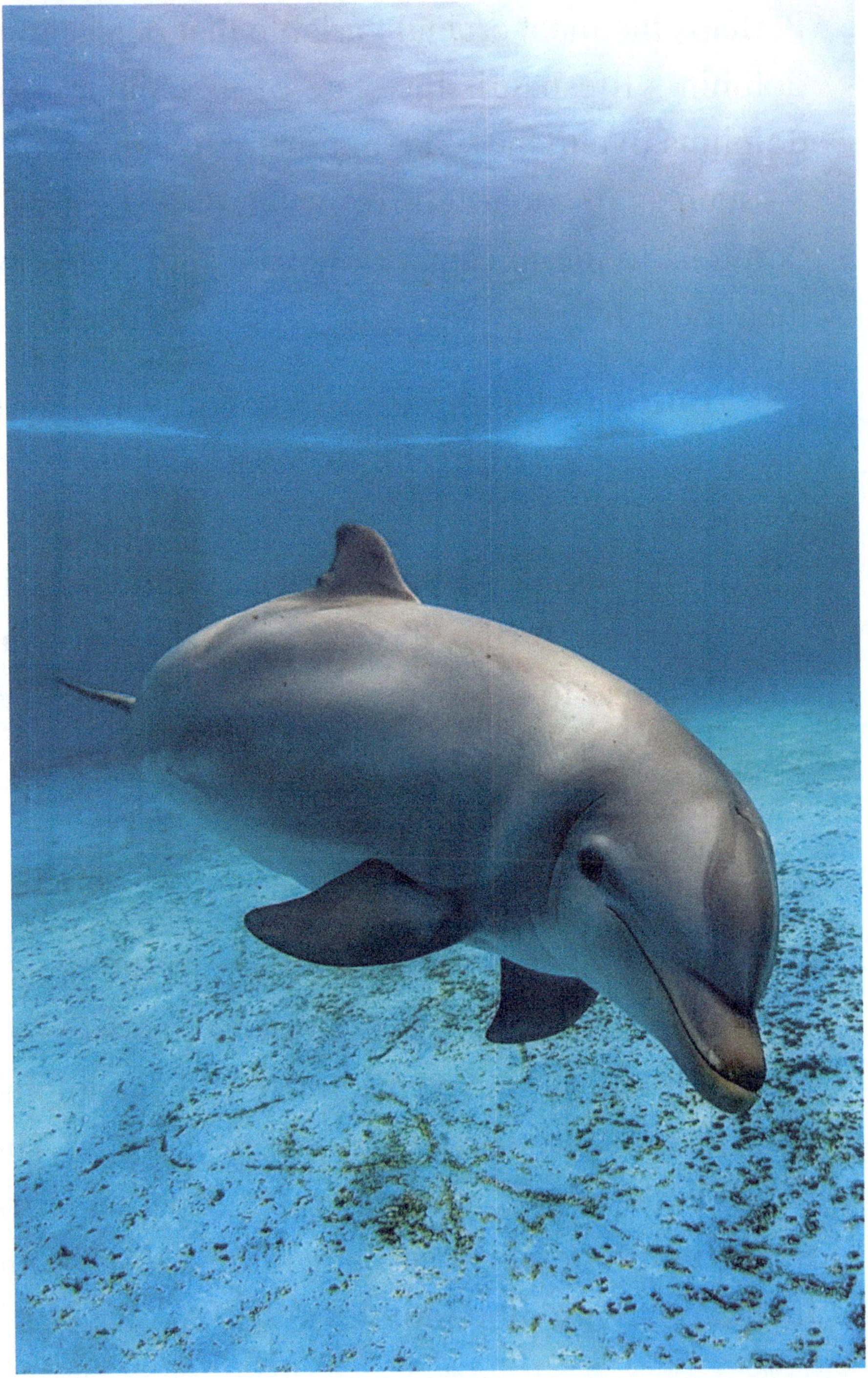

Additionally, the size of the dolphin's tank cannot compare with the immense size of the ocean. The dolphin might not be able to get as much exercise in captivity. Perhaps these factors contribute to their short lifespan.

Through the years, there have been significant improvements to the conditions of aquariums. As a result, some captive dolphins live a bit longer.

On a happier note, the world's oldest orca (affectionately known as "**Granny**") was reported to have lived for an incredible 105 years! She lived in the wild, off the coast of British Columbia and Washington State. She was said to have been born in 1911 and died in 2016.

Imagine all the world events that she lived through!

"Granny" and her family were the subject of many dolphin studies, and scientists were able to learn a great deal about orcas from her.

Do dolphins have any predators?

Dolphins have a couple of natural predators; **sharks** and **orcas** are the only two creatures that hunt them. Remember, an orca is a dolphin. But orcas have been known to eat their own kind. They might feed on the *common dolphin*, the *dusky dolphin*, and the *hourglass dolphin*.

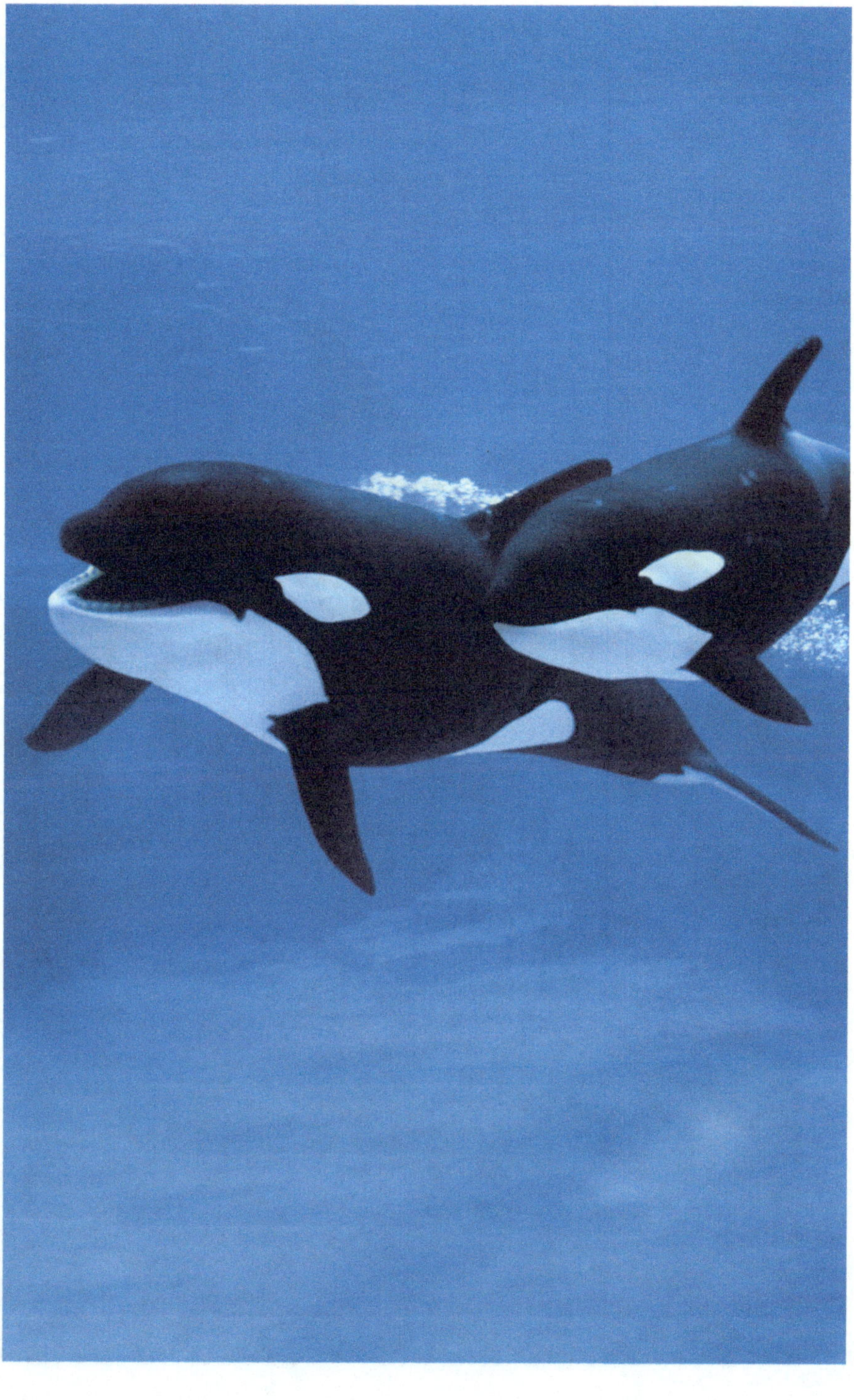

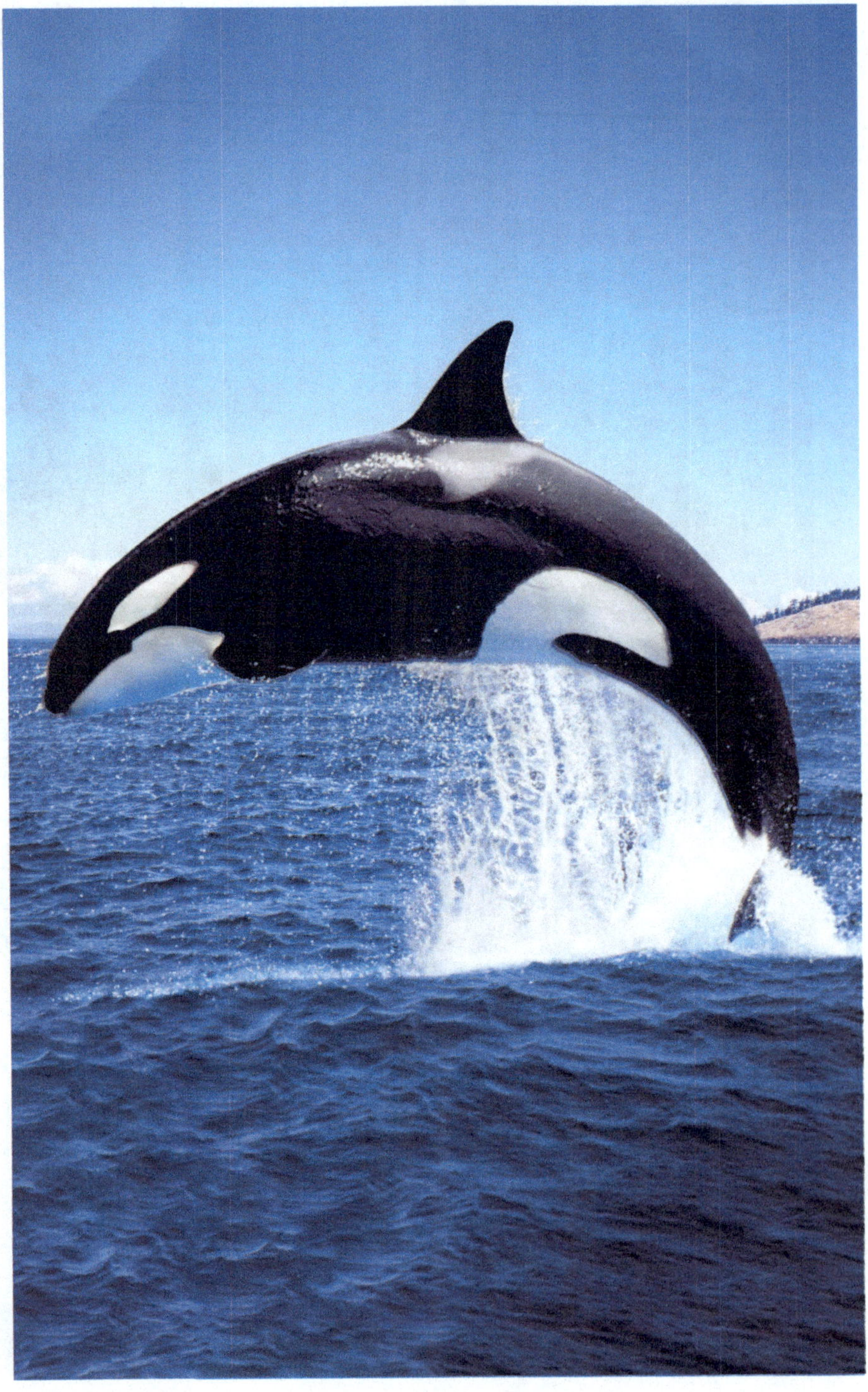

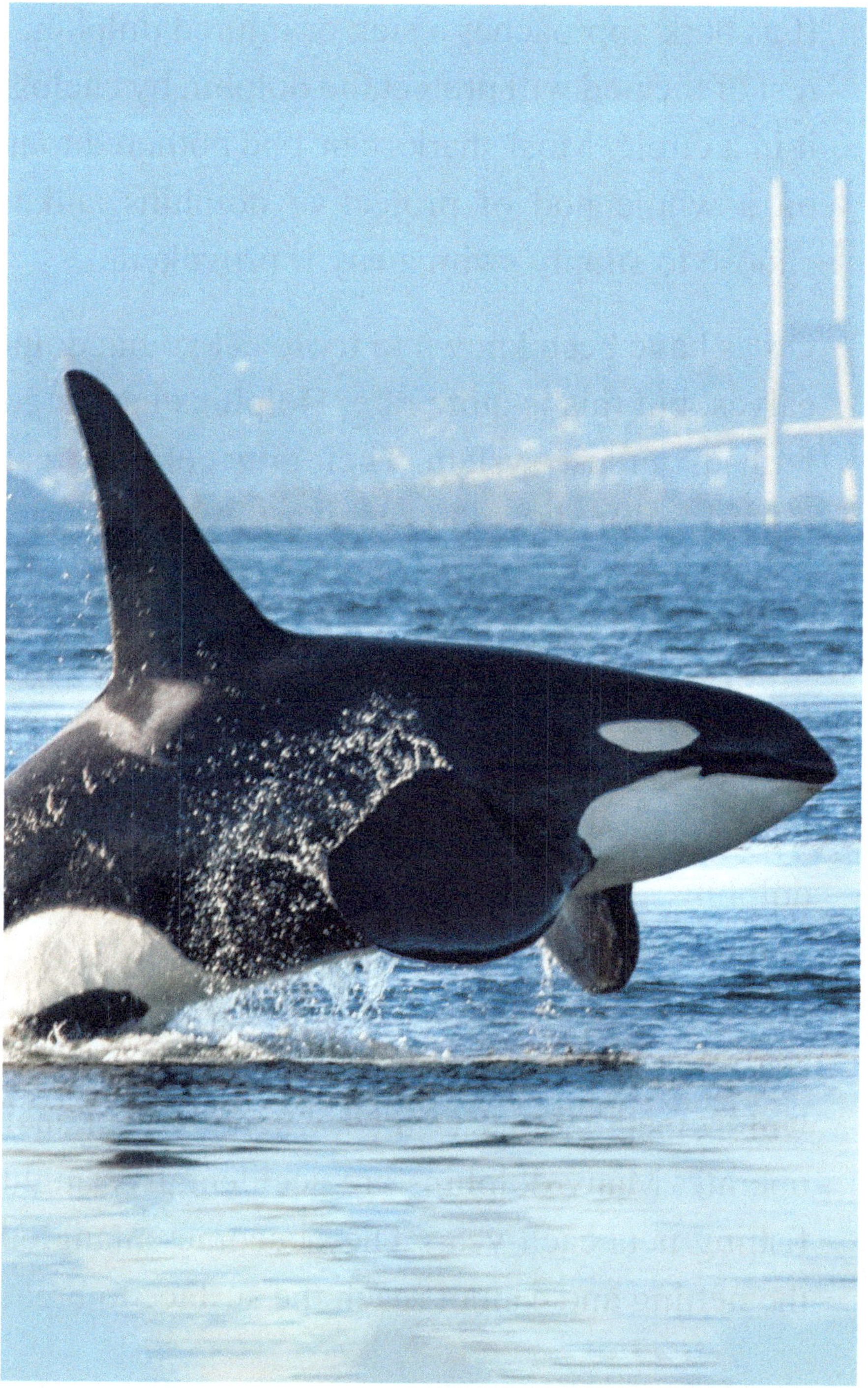

If a shark approaches a sick or injured dolphin, the rest of the pod will protect the dolphin by enclosing it in a circle. Most sharks can't be bothered to take on a whole pod of protective dolphins and will choose to simply swim away if provoked.

Orcas have been known to try to eat young dolphin calves, but this is quite rare. Dolphins have a good built-in defense system. Their gray coloring makes it hard for predators to see them. And they have a thick layer of **blubber** (or fat) surrounding their vital organs from attack.

So, when it comes to natural predators of the wild, dolphins don't have much to worry about. Instead, it is humans who have made life challenging for the dolphins. In fact, humans are considered the dolphin's most treacherous predator. This is primarily because dolphins enjoy swimming in the shallow waters where fish are abundant. Unfortunately, this is also where large fisheries operate. Many dolphins are accidentally caught in fishing nets each year. They become entangled in the netting and cannot reach the surface to breathe.

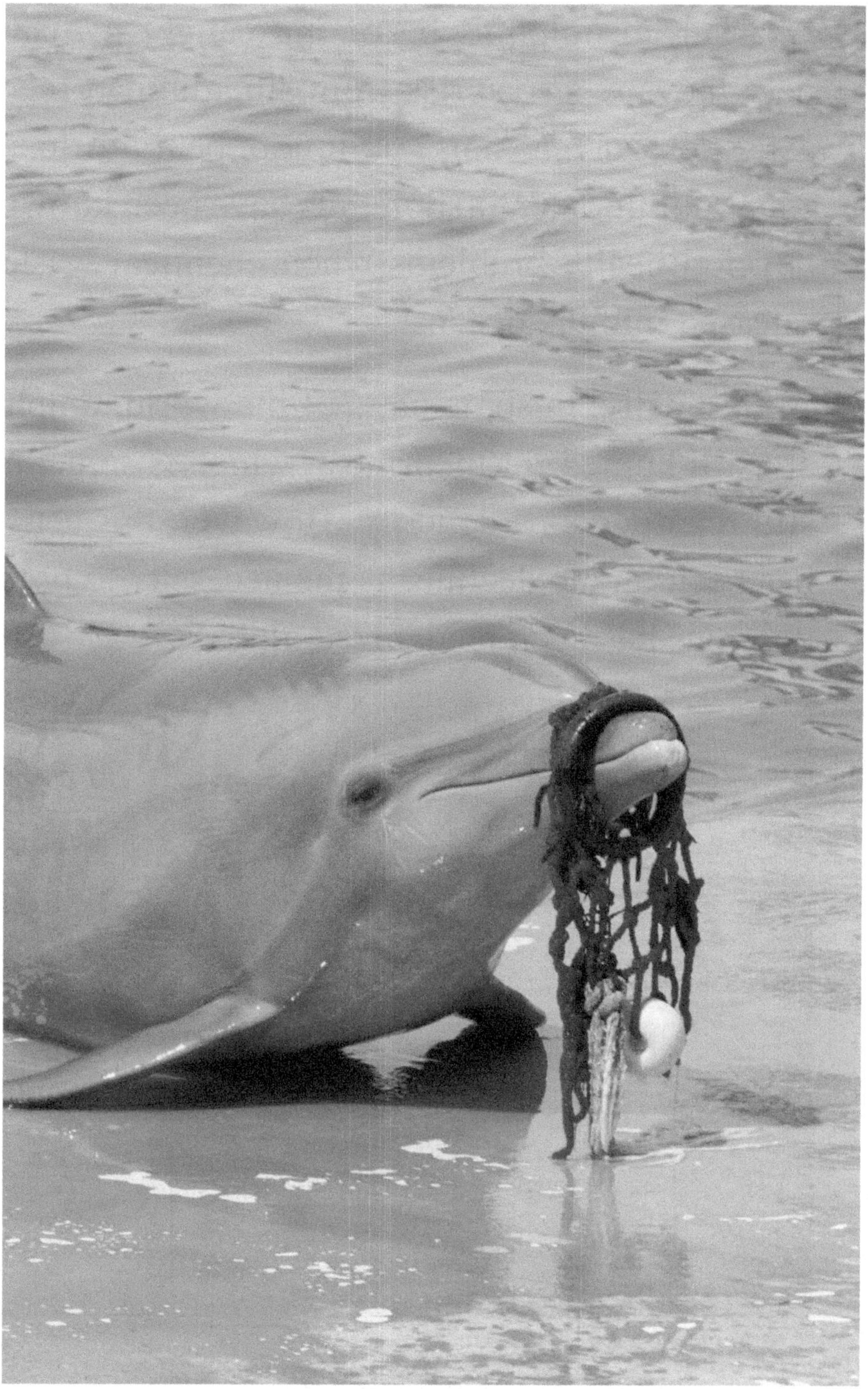

Apart from dolphins becoming caught in fishing nets, they are also at risk from other human-related activities, such as noise pollution, boat traffic, and water pollution. Wild dolphins have been known to develop health problems when chemical waste is released into the oceans.

Additionally, in some parts of the world, dolphins are still hunted for their meat, which is sometimes still regarded as a delicacy. However, this activity has been on the decline, as the necessity to protect dolphins has been recognized globally.

Are dolphins endangered?

There are a lot of dolphins in the world. Nevertheless, some dolphin species are at risk of becoming **endangered** or **extinct**. According to the IUCN *(International Union for Conservation of Nature)*, there are four species of dolphins that are classified as *critically endangered*. These are the *Maui dolphin*, *Hector's dolphin*, the *Ganges River dolphin*, and the *Indus River dolphin*.

You can see a *Hector's dolphin* on the next page. Note its unique blowhole.

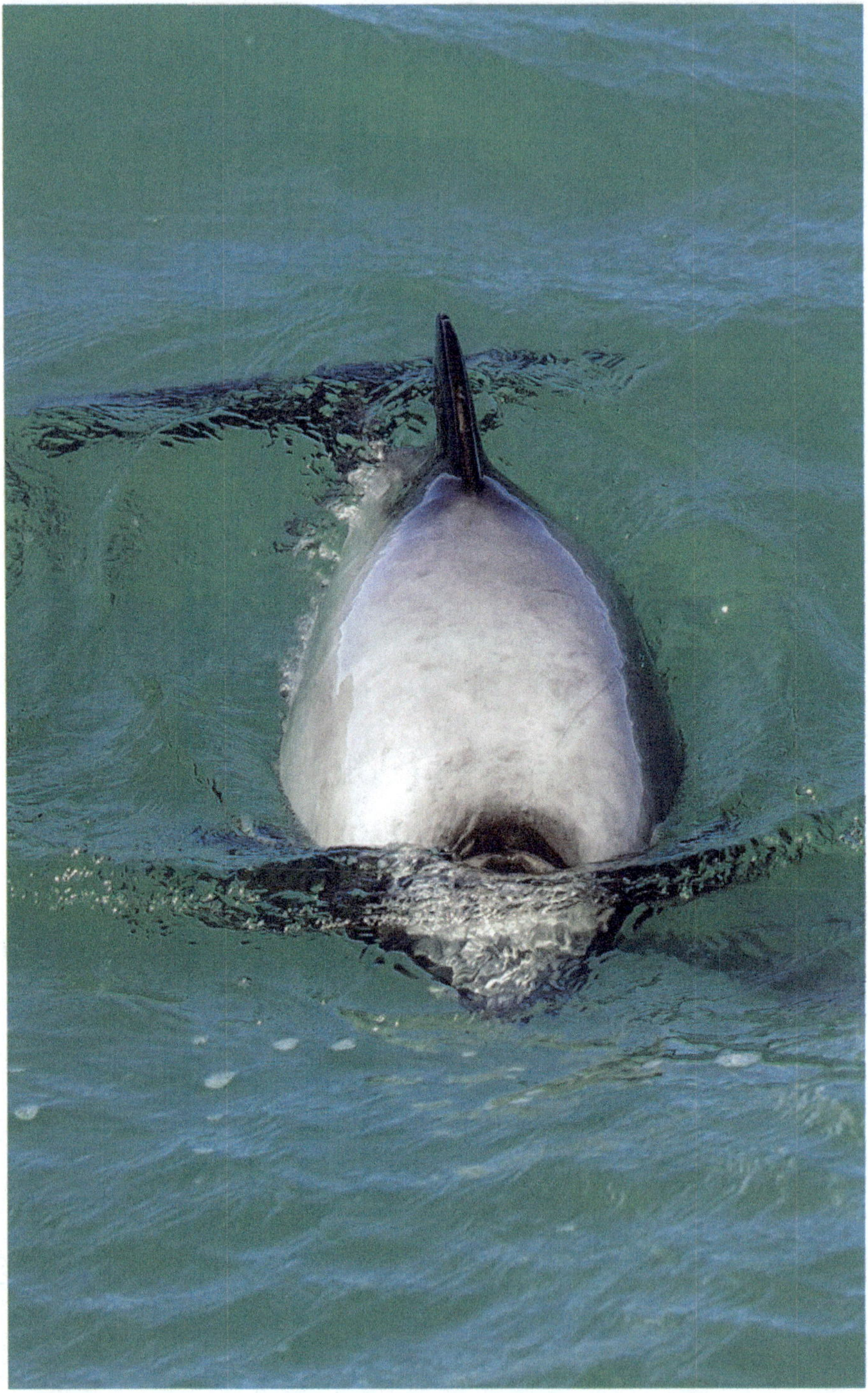

Several other dolphin species are considered to be either **threatened** or **vulnerable** — primarily due to habitat loss, water pollution, over-fishing, climate change, and other human activities.

Fortunately, conservation efforts have been put in place to protect and save these beautiful creatures. Many conservationists and animal welfare groups are working hard to raise awareness of the plight of the dolphin.

By taking the time to educate ourselves about these magnificent animals, we hope to build a better understanding of dolphins and the many threats they face. Hopefully, in reading books like this, you will be better equipped to share this information with others and help to raise awareness about dolphin conservation around the world. By learning as much as we can about their behavior, their habitats, and their needs, we can work to ensure that dolphins will be around for many generations to come.

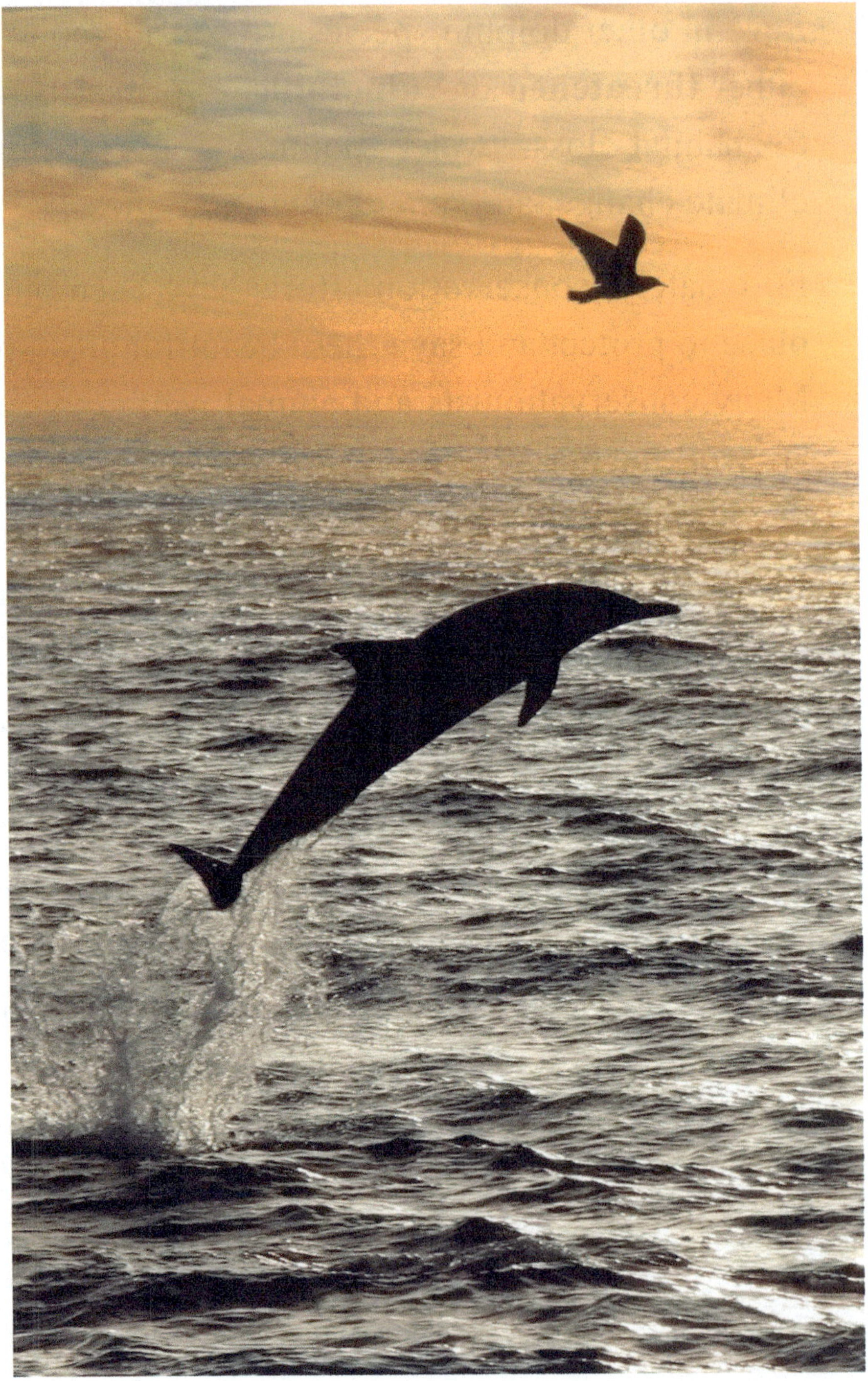

Did you like the book?

Thank you so much for reading our book! We hope we've been able to inspire you to learn more about our wonderful world of animals. If you get a moment, please consider leaving us a book review at Amazon. We're a small family company and for us, book reviews mean *everything*. Your support helps us to spread the message about animal education and conservation. Have a blessed day!

Animal Fact Finders

Maze Game

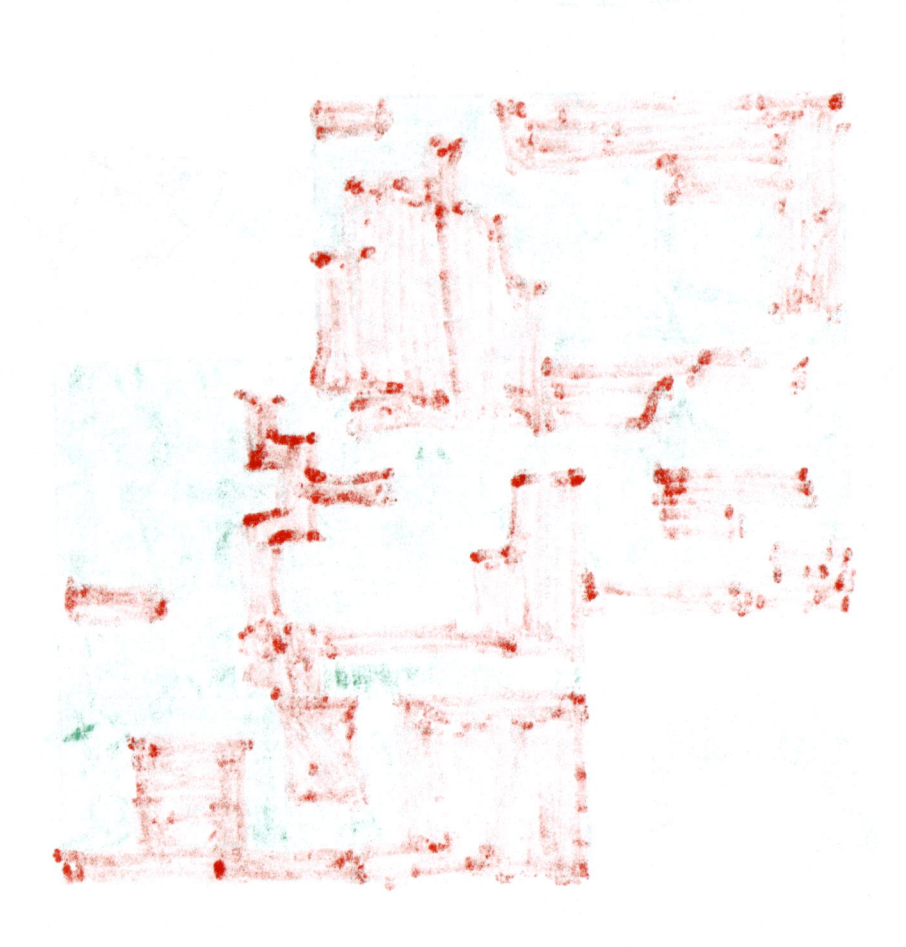

Made in the USA
Las Vegas, NV
19 April 2024